# OMG! WTF?

## OMG! What's The Focus?

**A Guide for Building an Actionable Business Plan**

FORD KYES    BARB KYES    JULIET KYES

Published by Richter Publishing LLC    www.richterpublishing.com

Copyright © 2014 Kyes Kreative Holdings

Edited by: Casey Cavanagh, Ricardo Angulo & Ke'Shawnda

ISBN: 0692443290
ISBN-13: 9780692443293

## PRAISE FOR **OMG! WHAT'S THE FOCUS?**

"For any current or future business owner willing to work for success, *OMG! What's the Focus* is priceless. The Kyes show you how to set or reset fundamental goals, establish the elements of a sound organization, and ultimately create a profitable enterprise!"

– **Marshall Goldsmith** author or editor of 35 books including the global bestsellers <u>MOJO</u> and <u>What Got You Here Won't Get You There</u>.

"Coaching and planning in business is no longer an option. It's an imperative if you're seeking to win in today's competitive marketplace. This book provides the "Kyes" for your success."

– **Jeffrey Gitomer,** *Author of <u>The Little Red Book of Selling</u> - The #1 best-selling sales book of all time*

"Anyone who knows me, knows that I preach focus, planning and accountability for small business success. I am so happy to find a book by Ford, Barb & Juliet Kyes that preaches the same philosophy. Better yet, in their new book, **OMG! WTF?**, they guide you step by step through a focused plan of attack. Add this book to your business library, read it and follow its suggestions and you'll be further ahead on your journey towards business success."

– **Dr. Tony Alessandra,** *Hall-of-Fame Keynote Speaker and author of <u>The Platinum Rule for Small Business Success</u>*

"If you're not achieving the business goals you had hoped to (let's face it, that's 90% of businesses) then OMG! WTF? will get you on track and heading in the right direction. I have personally worked with the Kyes and guarantee that if you put the knowledge of Ford, Barb and Juliet into action you will see some amazing results! OMG! WTF? is easy to read and even easier to put into Action! If you want to earn more, you have to LEARN MORE, having this book on your reading list is a must!"

– **Ben Fewtrell** *- CEO ActionCOACH ANZ, Keynote Speaker, Author and Host to the popular Business Brain Food Podcast.*

FORD KYES     BARB KYES     JULIET KYES

"OMG! INTBALTA (Oh My God/I Needed This Book A Long Time Ago!). In more than 35 years of working for and with many companies in developing branding and marketing strategies, I have learned that the truly successful brands are those that have a clear focus on what they need to do to differentiate themselves from the competition and provide true value to their customers.  The other companies that flounder or have disappeared from the marketplace suffered from the tendency to take a shotgun approach to their marketing and strategies that left them all over the board and irrelevant to their target customers.  In this book, the Kyes not only clearly define why having a precise focus is critical to success, but they also provide the tools and procedures to keep your business plan and your goals in line with your unique selling proposition.  Sharing important perspectives from some of the best in the business experts as well as from their own experiences, Barb, Juliet and Ford bring your quest for a focused approach to the business to life and jumpstart your organization on the road to success.  OMG! WTF?  is an important book for any business with a sound concept.  Moreover, it will be invaluable to any manager who wants a successful life as well."

– **Ken Banks**, *CEO, KAB Marketing, former SVP for Marketing at PetSmart, Circuit City, Eckerd Drug and Doner Advertising*


"I have personally worked with the Kyes as a client and have engaged them to work with my executive team for the past four years.  I can tell you first hand, this team of coaches definitely understands and knows how to transfer the power of focus to businesses.  Their new book, OMG! WTF? What's the focus? provides the practical advice any business owner needs to manage their business with the focus that is essential for success. If you want great insights you can implement tomorrow, put this book on your reading list and prepare to take notes! Coaching has been a core element in my business and personal life (as an Olympic athlete and as a player and then coach on the 1978 and 1979 Alabama National Championship teams under Coach Bear Bryant). These 3 coaches have really put together a great playbook for the business owner wanting to win!"

– **Dewey Mitchell,** *Broker/Owner, Berkshire Hathaway HS Florida Properties Group*

"Coming from Australia to the US, the Kyes were some of the first people my family met. Early on I understood their business model and how they operated as amazing coaches. Their knowledge and methods have tied in perfectly with this compelling book. OMG! WTF? , which covers so much valuable information for business whether you are starting up or are a seasoned entrepreneur. I recommend this book to the people that are serious about results and getting their business in top gear! Happy days!"

— **Anthony Amos,** *Multi-founding Franchisor / Speaker / Co-Author of How to Catch a Shark with Kevin Harrington from Shark Tank*

"The Kyes have written the ultimate "How To" handbook about business ownership and management. OMG! WTF? is an easy read for busy business people, written in a way that allows you to quickly find the focus area you're concerned about, and get the practical advice you need. It has tremendously helpful specifics and no theory. It's a drivers' manual for those in the drivers' seat. I have known the Kyes for 8 years and they're among the very best business driving instructors you can find. Read this and reach out to them before you crash!"

— **Nick Dove,** *Managing Partner & CEO of ActionCOACH OneCo (business coaching master franchise in 41 States of North America)*

"Most talk about growing their business. Few are willing to do what it takes to systematically evolve their business. If you are a serious business owner and you are willing to do more than just read a book, then OMG! WTF? is the book for you. The authors have built one of the most successful business coaching practices in the United States and this book will give a peek behind the curtain. It may just be one of the most important books you read."

— **Rick Bisio,** *Franchise Coach and Author of The Educated Franchisee*

"This book lays the foundation for more than just creating a successful business, it is an outline that can be applied to all aspects of our lives just by changing a few words and applying it to a need or problem. This should be a must read for all seniors graduating from high school or college. We all come out of school full of excitement and possibilities but without a plan to approach how we will go about applying what we have learned or think we know! The Kyes team explains the why and the how! OMG! WTF? makes manageable what I didn't previously think I could understand. Do you want to reach a bigger audience or understand why your business is not reaching its fullest potential?  Then read this book carefully and you will have ah-ha moments that will open the path for your way forward."

– **Alex E. Cramer,** *CFO, Capstone Tropical Holdings, Inc and Berkshire Hathaway HomeServices, FPG.*

"Lots of great and oftentimes missed ideas for entrepreneurs to consider as they grow their businesses.  The Kyes did a nice job of combining psychology with business school basics in an easy-to-read format."

– **Bryan Spaulding**, *CEO, Spaulding Group, Inc.*

"Fast read, actionable advice, and I love the one-page worksheets at the end of each chapter! There are some items included that could really make an impact on businesses... if followed through on, of course ;-)."

– **Daniel James Scott**, *Executive Director, Tampa Bay Technology Forum and 2013 Association for Small Business and Entrepreneurship "Educator of the Year" award recipient.*

"OMG! WTF?  is spot on with business owners.  The Kyes team brings the best thinking on the how's, why's, and what's of focus and planning to the world of business owners. Every business owner can use this book as a tool to build upon their mindset, their productivity, marketing, sales, team, how to manage change, and more importantly focus their efforts to gain clarity on what is important to improve and achieve their daily goals in business and personal life. Barb, Ford and Juliet has written the perfect recipe for today's loss of attention for business and life...FOCUS and PLANNING. It has been an honor over the past 8 years to have seen Barb, Ford and Juliet grow into the most AMAZING business coaches and see them make a huge impact on business owners and their community. It is a true honor to personally call them my friend and wish them much success on their first book."

– **Angie Fairbanks**, *Chief Global Community Officer of ActionCOACH*

"It is not often that one book sums up all the keys to being successful in business and OMG! What's The Focus? is definitely one of those exceptional books. The Kyes have covered a complete spectrum from ways to train ourselves to think about success, practical outlines of business building strategies, even understanding accounting all the way through to material to download and use immediately. What's more everything covered in this book is simply outlined and is based on a solid foundation of years of real-time business and coaching experience so we can have 100% confidence it's been proven to work over and over again. I believe that using even a fraction of the knowledge gained from OMG! WTF?, a reader will make huge advances - I am putting this book on my compulsory client reading list!"

– **Bruce Wilson**, *Global Master Coach, Licensed ActionCOACH Business Coach*

"A great book with all the KEYS to build an awesome business! If everyone would just read, and then do, what the Kyes team details in OMG! What's The Focus? there would be so much more wealth and we could reach the vision of ActionCOACH, "World abundance through business re-education". Great work Team Kyes!"

– **Doug Winnie**, *Certified Million Dollar ActionCOACH*

# DEDICATION

*Notice when "A" happens and you do "B" - "C" always follows. Next time "A" happens and you choose a different response than "B", you can be sure "C" will not happen.*

❖

*If you've never been on fire, you can't burnout.*

We want to dedicate the book to our tremendous mentor and role model, Joan Kyes, R.N., MSN (collectively, our mother, grandmother, best friend and coach). At the time of her retirement, Joan was an Assistant Professor of Psychiatry in the School of Medicine and in the School of Nursing at the University of Pittsburgh as well as the Associate Administrator (and Director of Nursing) for the world famous Western Psychiatric Institute and Clinic in Pittsburgh. She authored the most popular psychiatric textbook for nurses globally through two editions (published by Lippincott). She was one of only a handful of women at the University of Pennsylvania in the 1960's to attend the Wharton School where she received a minor in business administration while completing her Master's Degree in psychiatric nursing.

In addition to all of her responsibilities at Pitt, she presented an average of 75 keynote presentations per year for over 10 years for businesses as well as hospitals all over the US and Canada. All of her accomplishments as a career-minded women in the 60's and 70's, including all of her college education were accomplished after she returned from service in a MASH Unit in Korea and while raising and supporting a son as a single mom. Her consistently positive view on life and can-do attitude was an inspiration to all who knew her.

# DISCLAIMER

This book is designed to provide information on business coaching only. This information is provided and sold with the knowledge that the publisher and author do not offer any legal or medical advice. In the case of a need for any such expertise, consult with the appropriate professional. This book does not contain all information available on the subject. This book has not been created to be specific to any individual's or organization's situation or needs. Every effort has been made to make this book as accurate as possible. However, there may be typographical and/ or content errors. Therefore, this book should serve only as a general guide and not as the ultimate source of subject information. This book contains information that might be dated and is intended only to educate and entertain. The author and publisher shall have no liability or responsibility to any person or entity regarding any loss or damage incurred, or alleged to have incurred, directly or indirectly, by the information contained in this book. You hereby agree to be bound by this disclaimer or you may return this book within the guarantee time period for a full refund. In the interest of full disclosure, this book contains affiliate links that might pay the author or publisher a commission upon any purchase from the company. While the author and publisher take no responsibility for the business practices of these companies and or the performance of any product or service, the author or publisher has used the product or service and makes a recommendation in good faith based on that experience. Any and all references to methods by Brad Sugars and Action Coaches, is owned solely by them. This is just a reference guide to teach others how to utilize their system.

# CONTENTS

FOREWORD..................................................................xvii

INTRODUCTION .........................................................xxiii

**CHAPTER 1 -** ATTITUDE ........................................ 25

**CHAPTER 2 -** SIX STEPS ...................................... 49

**CHAPTER 3 -** PRODUCTIVITY ............................... 63

**CHAPTER 4 -** FINANCIALS.................................... 79

**CHAPTER 5 -** MARKETING ................................... 105

**CHAPTER 6 -** SALES ............................................ 135

**CHAPTER 7 -** SYSTEMS ....................................... 149

**CHAPTER 8 -** TEAM............................................... 159

**CHAPTER 9 -** PLANNING ..................................... 1733

**CHAPTER 10 -** ACCOUNTABILITY........................ 185

ABOUT THE AUTHORS.............................................. 193

FINAL THOUGHTS ................................................... 205

# FOREWORD

I really got to know Ford and Barb Kyes when they came to their 11-day intensive franchise training in 2007. Fortunately, they had me as their speaker for the first and final day. The Kyes were the third "firm" model in the US in those days with no other firm or coach in their specific market. They have done an amazing job bringing the ActionCOACH brand image to the Tampa Bay region in a few short years.

The title of their first book, *OMG! WTF?* has hit the nail on the head for business owners. Business owners have a passion or a really great idea and they think that they know how to run a business. They get into business and say, "**O**h **M**y **G**od! What was I thinking?" They are now wearing all of the hats in their business, working 7 days a week, 10 or more hours a day, putting out fires. The Kyes team is really great at helping business owners get to "**W**hat's **T**he **F**ocus?", by sitting them down, strategically helping them plan out the future of their business and getting agreement of a focused plan of attack. They help the owners understand the difference in having a REAL business that is saleable and works without the owner having to be there day in and day out...versus one that is truly just a job which is also known as **J**ust **O**ver **B**roke.

FORD KYES     BARB KYES     JULIET KYES

After reading this book, I believe business owners and executives will get incredible clarity on what is the focus when it comes to the critical items required to improve their businesses and their lives. The Kyes team was able to incorporate the teachings of ActionCOACH and optimized our planning process with what they have learned over the last 8 years in business working with over 70 different types of businesses in their market.

If you follow along, you will find many actionable items to get you started and prepared for the coaching process with one of my top teams in this global franchise!

Look, if you've been growing your business for several years now and you still have to be there almost every day, or you are working too many hours each week, or you are taking the least amount of pay and vacations each year – then it's time to figure out what IS YOUR focus. Put this book at the top of you reading list and contact the Kyes team to get the accountability to take action today so you will have that saleable business in your future!

All my best!
Bradley Sugars
Founder of ActionCOACH
Chairman of the Board, ActionCOACH

# ACKNOWLEDGMENTS

We would like to thank our clients for helping us make this book a reality. You push us to grow and excel! We are so grateful you gifted us with the opportunity to be a positive force in your life and business. You inspire this book and are the reason we are still in business today.

We would also like to thank our mentors: Brad Sugars, Verne Harnish, Jeffrey Gitomer, Marshall Goldsmith, Keith Cunningham, Jay Conrad Levinson, and Dr. Tony Alessandra.

And of course our coaches: Ben Fewtrell, Bruce Wilson, Andrew Johnston, Chuck Kocher, Nick Dove and the other thousand plus who abundantly share information on our internal forum and at our ActionCOACH conferences.

# INTRODUCTION

Business owners who are new to being coached and having a plan always have a lot in common in the way they operate and struggle to find focus. This book is a collaboration of three coaches who have worked directly with business owners in the last several years assisting them with putting their goals on paper and creating a lasting impact on the growth of their businesses.

This book is meant to serve as a guide to assist you in forming an operational plan for your company. A specifically targeted, goal oriented plan that both engages and inspires you—something you can compile all on one sheet of paper to run your weekly schedule based on your future annual and 90 day goals. Once your focus and a clear plan is set in place with your team, attaining the results you want will happen much quicker than it has in the past for your business.

*"I don't focus on what I'm up against. I focus on my goals and try to ignore the rest."*
**- Venus Williams, Tennis Legend and Olympic Champion**

*"You can focus on things that are barriers or you can focus on scaling the wall or redefining the problem."*
**- Tim Cook, CEO, Apple**

# 1

## Attitude

*"Nothing can stop the man with the right mental attitude from achieving his goal; nothing on earth can help the man with the wrong mental attitude."* - **Thomas Jefferson**

You may be wondering why Attitude would be the first chapter in a book about the most important areas on which to focus in your business. It's intentional. Whatever you focus upon increases! If you focus on what you don't have, you'll keep seeing more things you don't have. But if you focus on your future vision and on what you need to do each day to bring that vision into your present (future/present thinking), you will find the resources (internally and externally) to achieve that vision.

Regardless of the type of business – and we've worked with over 70 distinctly different types of businesses since 2007 - CPAs, lawyers, architects, pest control company, mold/water damage company, carpet cleaners, banks, large ship repair company, doctors, pharmacies, printers, international exporters, restaurants just to name a few. The owner's willingness to take personal responsibility, accountability and ownership to succeed (no matter what) is the most critical factor to exceptional performance. As Henry Ford famously said: "Whether you think you can or you think you can't, you're right." He also said: "One of the greatest discoveries a man makes, one of his great surprises, is to find he can do what he was afraid he couldn't." Your mindset upon waking up every day and being willing to establish and commit to new routines and habits, will determine your ability to perform - to focus on each element for success described in this book.

There are hundreds, of research studies, books and audio CDs on the subject of the importance of keeping your attitude and mindset positive. The first big question is: "Why should I do this?" The second is: "How?"

How many people do you know who have an attitude that seems negative, no matter what day it is or where you meet them? This type of personality can drain the energy of an entire room. Negative thoughts are like a virus; they move in, replicate and attempt to take over a healthy host. Positive thoughts and attitudes are the antidote and can spread just as quickly.

But that's just the way it is, right? Why should I work on my mindset and focus on a positive attitude? In a 2005 Meta-Analysis (published in the Psychological Bulletin) of over 200 studies involving nearly 275,000 subjects showed unequivocally that a positive mindset leads to improved performance (success) in virtually every aspect of our lives but especially at work. Optimistic sales people, for example, outsell their pessimistic counterparts by 56% and doctors in a positive mood make accurate diagnosis 19% faster.

Frankly, we can't keep a terrific attitude every second of the day, every day. We all have upsetting or distracting events that occur throughout our day. The trick lies in how quickly we choose to catch ourselves and turn our attitudes around.

Keeping a positive attitude is a choice. Positive people read different books, they listen to different things in their car while driving. They regularly and actively review those things for which they are grateful. They hang out with other positive people and they hire only positive people in their company – you get the drift. They take personal responsibility for factors they can control to make it easier to stay positive.

Let us be very clear here. You can read this book, work hard at applying it in your business or career and still not achieve the level of success you wished because you did not substantially change your mental approach. If you are truly open to change, the results you achieve will know no bounds. Focus first (and always) on "raising your BAR":

**B** - who you are **BE**ing
**A** - **A**ctions you choose to take
**R** - the **R**esults you achieve

Who are you being? Do you portray an attitude that attracts success? What words do others use to describe you when you are not around? Do you bring energy into a room or has your business situation worn you down? Do you have habits every day that raise your game or slow you down?

To use an old farming analogy: "You can use all the tools you want, but nothing will grow on soil that isn't properly prepared." If you're open to change and learning best practices, that is fertile ground.

When we talk about the title of this book, *OMG! What's The Focus?*, it brings to mind the teachings of Daniel Goleman in his book *Focus: The Hidden Driver of Excellence*. Daniel Goleman, a science writer for the NY Times, was the first to popularize the early research on *Emotional Intelligence.*   According to Goleman, there are three types of focus.

The *Inner Focus* which has to do with your self-awareness, managing your intuition, choosing your positive self-talk and choosing your attitude. It raises the question that if you are not aware and you don't know what you don't know about yourself, how can you ever improve and manage yourself? Whatever you focus on will become your reality. The more you see and look for negative situations in your life and business, the more you will find them. It's like the example of when your employees are late for work and have excuses or reasons. You as the business owner begin to doubt that any of your employees will ever be free of late excuses and are labeled "always late". We will talk about this later in the Covey concept of E + R = O and choosing your outcome to events.

The second is *Focus on Others.* When we are aware that we are focusing on the needs of others, we are more likely to BE in a supportive state.  When we focus on others, our relationships become much smoother and we gain the sense that we are participating in the needs of others to help them be successful in life and business. This attunement to others improves communication and the opportunity for alignment of their goals with the organization's goals. Focus on others and noticing our impact on the emotions of others, positions us to become a "bucket filler" (as in *How Full is Your Bucket* by Tom Rath) to increase the positive energy and engagement of the team. Adversely, a "bucket scooper", is one who takes from people in terms of their positive emotions by consistently giving negative comments creating an environment which is not conducive to engagement and productivity. In the "Full Bucket" environment our sense of wellbeing is enhanced and we rise to the state of appreciation because the people around us are fully aware of others' emotional needs.

The third is *Outer Focus.* In this focus, you are aware and attend to the greater environment in the world, the political scope of your organization or even global community and what role you play in it. When we understand all three of these focuses, we are able to contribute at a higher level of focus that helps us create success and amazing productivity in life, our relationships, our passionate calling, and our work!

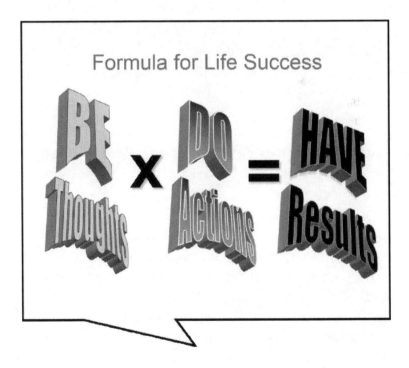

Bradley J. Sugars, founder and current chairman of the board of ActionCOACH, built a basic formula to achieve a successful life:

# BE x DO = HAVE

Most people get the formula backwards. They think: "If I had a million dollars, I would BE able to DO what I need to do to succeed and HAVE  all the  things I want (and then I would be "Happy"). But think about lottery winners. Suddenly, they win over a million dollars, and for a while it seems like they are on top of the world. But eventually, most end up struggling. Most lose all the money they won, because they do not know how to BE a millionaire or what to DO to make that kind of money last. Professional athletes also suffer from lack of knowledge about financial matters.

*"Sports Illustrated estimated in 2009 that 78 percent of NFL players are bankrupt or facing serious financial stress within two years of ending their playing careers and that 60 percent of NBA players are broke within five years of retiring from the game."*

*Quote from: http://usatoday30.usatoday.com/sports/story/2012-04-22/Pro-athletes-and-financial-trouble/54465664/1

They are similar to business owners and corporate executives who start businesses because they are great at a craft, calling, or trade but lack the skills to manage their money and put controls in place to assure that they are gaining a return.

It's okay to set clear future goals for the things you want to have in your life, but it's also very important to understand where you are and where you're going. What is your vision or future state? First you have to ask yourself, "Who should I become? What kind of person (skills, knowledge, attitude, beliefs, etc.) would naturally DO the things necessary to achieve my goals? Basically, who do I need to BE?" Jim Rohn, author of *Five Major Pieces to the Life Puzzle*, once said, "Work harder on yourself than you do on your business. If you work hard on your business, you can earn a living. Work hard on yourself, you can earn a fortune." If you want to earn more, you need to learn more –it's that simple!

In order to achieve, you must understand your personal development needs, your attitude, and who you are "being" - the "BE" part of the formula. But who exactly are you? Think of yourself as an iceberg. When you see an iceberg, what you can actually see is only above the surface of the water - a white, shiny object floating by - but under the surface there is enough substance to sink a boat like the Titanic. This is a great analogy for each of us as well. What people can directly observe is that persona we create and display—at least, that is what's visible. But below the surface is what makes up the majority of an iceberg and a person, so to speak.

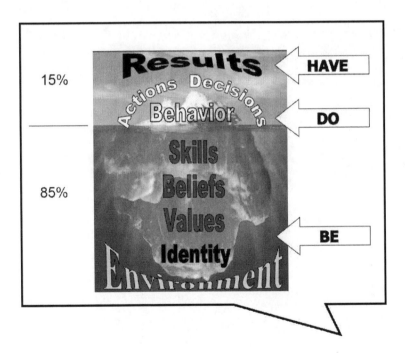

What appears on your surface is the persona you create, the actions and behaviors you display (both positive and negative) and the results you achieve. Your persona and results, however, are greatly impacted by factors below the surface - your "BE". So if you want to change your decisions, actions, behaviors and results, the first thing you should do is work on your "BE", which will require you to go below the surface level.

Just below the surface are our skills (and knowledge). One of the easiest and most common ways to improve our ability to DO is to improve our skills and knowledge. As you think about your dreams and goals (what you are choosing to HAVE), begin to develop an inventory of the skills and knowledge you will need to effectively DO what will likely be needed to achieve that end result.

*Here is an ad example of beliefs of the past. Very Interesting? Who knew that doctors would smoke openly and guide Americans to smoke Camels?*

Deeper underneath lie our beliefs. Now, beliefs are really interesting because we will not take actions that are counter to our beliefs. If we don't believe something is possible for us, we won't even attempt it. What is a belief? It's something we hold to be true but is not necessarily true. Think back. We used to believe smoking cigarettes was cool. Everybody smoked all the time at restaurants, at offices—ashtrays were even once built into the hand rest in airplanes! Everybody we saw was smoking: news anchors, actors, and actresses, even doctors and nurses. We *believed* this was okay. When seatbelts first came out, many people believed they were dangerous. "Who wants to be trapped in a car? I want to make sure I get thrown clear of the car if an accident happens!" Now consider how differently society views these beliefs today. Just because we believe something, doesn't make it true, and beliefs can change. In fact, we can change our beliefs at any time (and often do). Once we decide, it can be instantaneous!

In reality, many of the beliefs we have often hold us back from making better decisions and from building a better business or life. Business owners often say to us, "I'm not good at math." If you believe that, it's unlikely you will develop financial skills. And in business, financials are the scorecard. If you can't keep score, you won't know the winners from the losers. If anyone is smart enough to enter the business world, they're smart enough to understand the financials. If you believe you're not good at math and won't ever be able to understand the financials, then you're never going to. You won't do the work to figure it out.

Let's dig deeper under that iceberg. Below skills and beliefs, are our values, identity, and finally environment. Values are your deep rooted ideals about what is good or bad and have a major influence on our perceptions of others and our attitude. It's critical to understand and articulate the definition of your most important values. Make sure your decisions align with your values. Make sure the people working with you are aligned with those values. Make sure your vendors, even your clients, are aligned with your values. When values align, we engage. We propel. We become much more motivated to do the hard work.

Finally, at the deepest level, the foundational piece of your iceberg: your identity. If you want to know what your identity is, pay attention to what you say to yourself about yourself when you're by yourself. That's your identity. Often times your self-talk is very negative. What are the things you're saying? "I'm not good at this, I'm not good at that, I can't do this, I can't do that..." That voice is just your brain interpreting your world around you to you (your deep consciousness that is observing the voice). You can control that voice and these statements can be changed to be positive. Here's a quick exercise to make the point: right now, have the voice inside your head say "hello" three times. Now have that voice yell "hello" three times – you can, in fact control that voice if you take time to notice it. Your self-talk will determine your *focus* and may be the single most important ingredient to your success.

Here's another great exercise: Sit down with a sheet of paper and draw a vertical line down the center. On the left half of the paper, write a list of everything your internal voice is saying (to yourself) that is negative. Pay attention for a few hours or a day and record the list of your most common negatives. Now thing, what would a counter, positive statement be for each? "I'm getting better at this every day, everything gets easier once you do it and practice it, I'm smart and can easily learn anything..." On the right half of your paper, next to each item on your "negative" list, write the opposing positive - then start repeating the positive statements every time you notice that internal voice saying the negative.

Lastly, think about your environment. What kind of environment are you in every day? Do you associate with negative people? Do you seek those with high energy and confidence (likely with great self-talk)? Do you realize that: "You are the average of the five people you spend the most time with" as Jim Rohn puts it? Something to consider, who are you choosing to hang out with? Ever notice when the wrong people leave your life, the right things start happening? Our clients report a huge difference when they choose learning, growing, positive environments.

Above the surface of the iceberg is what everyone sees. It's what you "DO" that surfaces as your actions, your decisions and your behaviors. It's what you "HAVE" that shows up as your results. This surface view of what you "DO" and "HAVE" is only 15% of the picture. The other 85% below the surface is where the biggest results originate from – adjustments there impact the root of the tree rather than just the seasonal leaves.

Usually when business owners tell us that they can't get to the next level, or can't get the results they want, the "roadblock" is their own thinking and identity. If you want new results, you must get new thinking!

You: "OK coach, let's assume I'm beginning to understand the importance of working on my BE – in particular my beliefs and identity, how do I go about changing that?" Coach: "I'm so glad you asked. Step one is becoming aware – noticing what your internal voice is saying and acknowledging that it may not be serving you in achieving your goals and dreams. Next is incorporating a mental workout routine to flush out the negative self-talk by creating an exercise routine of positive and empowering thoughts. At the same time, identify your top priorities for skills/knowledge development and document a personal development plan."

Here's a quick primer on the IVVM system but for more information, make sure you go to the link and download the full IVVM exercise format.

## IVVM
### Idealize — Visualize — Verbalize — Materialize

Idealization ... think about and then describe to yourself your most ideal life. What does it mean to you to be the best that you can be? What is the grandest version of the greatest vision you ever had about yourself? What is your perfect relationship, health, home, business, bank balance, legacy? What are your dreams in life? You can make dreams come true, but first you've got to have them ...

Visualization ... invest just 5 minutes each morning and 5 minutes in the evening with your eyes closed visualizing everything you have dreamt and thought about in your mind ... do this as if it's already real ... Make it as specific as you can ...

**V**erbalization ... Now use the power of the Word ... Speak your truth ... Voice your goals to loved ones, close friends ... Write them down ... Then make a list of 20 "I AM" statements about YOU – that is, your future self. Describe traits you want to build on and will need in order to become the person you want to BEcome, in order to DO the things you need to do, in order to HAVE and experience all the things you dream of ... State these out loud to yourself every day ...

**M**aterialization ... Now it's time to take ACTION ... Make a decision ... Implement the Plan ... Choose every day that what you dream of is yours... take that belief into what you're DOing every day. Go about DOing with energy and emotion, as one who is happy with who you are and what you have, while at the same time being eager for more.

Why do we encourage our clients to practice the IVVM exercise? Current psychology has proven that people that are more positive are more likely to be successful. It is especially important when running a business that the leader is positive and lifts up the other members of the team. When our clients take the IVVM exercise seriously, they have had amazing results in their business. Our concierge physician client, for example, started her practice in 2010 when there was very little understanding of the value of the model of having a physician available 24/7 by cell phone, text or email who focused on keeping patients healthy (vs. treating illness). In this physician practice model, patients pay an annual cash fee and the physician does not accept any insurance for the professional component of care. All of her colleagues told her it would never work but she continued to believe in her dream and visualized the future state of her business. She has been in coaching for over 5 years. She is about to expand her business into other fee for service offerings, move into a larger space and has hired her 4th employee - her husband, another physician, who has quit his job and is joining her practice. She is debt free and her 4 year results from coaching is a revenue increase of 233%. She is on track to reach her maximum concierge client volume in the next several months. She tells everyone who will listen that her daily IVVM exercise was one of the keys to this success and she teaches this technique to patients that are stuck in the "I can't do it" syndrome as well. IVVM is a great tool to change your identity and your beliefs in a positive, self-serving way.

**FREE RESOURCE DOWNLOAD**

IVVM Exercise
www.actioncoachtampabay.com/ivvm

Here's another exercise: picture somebody who you really admire. It could be anyone. Write down words that describe them. Then go back and look at those words. Do the words have to do with their skill, knowledge, or attitude?

We've done this exercise with thousands of people. The list is always 85-90% attitude. That's because attitude is what people first notice when they watch you operate. Attitude is what causes us to respect you. Attitude makes up 90% of the visible habits of great leaders. If you can improve your attitude, your chances for success will improve dramatically and so will your happiness in all areas of your life.

## OVERCOMING RESISTANCE TO CHANGE

How can you make changes? Humans are creatures of habit; it comes naturally to do what we have always done. Albert Einstein once said, "Our current thinking will always get us our current situation (our current results)." New results require new thinking. New thinking requires change. The key to improving your chances at success is learning how to implement change.

## *FORMULA FOR CHANGE....*

# (D x V) + F > R

## (DISSATISFACTION x VISION) + FIRST STEP > RESISTENCE

Resistance to change is a universal behavior. All great changes meet resistance. In fact, if there is no resistance then there is usually no real desire or commitment to change. As human beings, we have to figure out how to overcome this resistance. Perhaps counterintuitive, first we need notice and enhance our level of dissatisfaction (D) with our current state. Think about your dissatisfaction, whether it's in business or finances or some other aspect of life. You need to clearly identify what it is you want to change. If there is no dissatisfaction with our current state, why would we change?  "Everything's fine, I'm perfectly satisfied – leave me alone." This is a prime example of how low dissatisfaction causes complacency.

On the other hand, having very high dissatisfaction and zero vision that it could be better, just becomes hopelessness. "Why should I bother? That's just the way it is. My hands are tied. Oh well, maybe next year will be better. Maybe since I don't have clients that day, I'll take the day off." So once you're clear on your dissatisfaction with your results, you must have a vision (V) of your desired future state to motivate change. The clearer, the better your vision will be. Only when you really buy into that vision, will  you really believe it is possible. At this point, all you need is a First (F) step -  a plan to get started and the will to participate.

This is the time when many people give up. They become afraid of diving in headfirst. Reaching a high level of success or the risk of failure or the risk of other's judgement can be a cause for fear. But this type of fear is just an acronym: **F**alse **E**xpectations **A**ppearing **R**eal.

So, Why Do People Stay
Where They Are?

**F**alse **E**xpectations **A**ppearing **R**eal

A lot of times, these false expectations appear to be real. If you challenge yourself, you'll find you're not putting yourself in a life threatening situation. What's the worst that can happen if you participate? That fear holds people from their dreams and aspirations. It can be fear of the unknown, change, or even success!

## I KNOW

If anybody has been around a teenager, they understand the challenge of the "I know" attitude. "I already heard this, I know. I'm ready to conquer life. I don't need to read. I don't need school. Whatever, I'm not listening. I know that already." As we get older, we become more subtle, more quiet. The minute we think "I know," a wall goes up. You create an impossibility for yourself. You cannot take on new information or new learning, yet that new learning is where the new results come from!

Instead of thinking "I know" or "I've tried that before", change your response (in your mind) to *"Isn't that interesting?"* I know it sounds silly, but say it out loud with an inflection of curiosity. *"Isn't that interesting?"* It doesn't say, "I agree with you," or, "I'm going to go do that." It says it's interesting, making you stop and think. Questions will pop up. How did you come up with that? What led you to that thinking? Why did you make that choice? How <u>could</u> that apply to my situation? You'll be blown away at how many important insights are waiting for you when you stop focusing on defending right or wrong and start opening your mind to possibility.

Be curious and ask yourself questions. Be interested in learning more. It will change the way you think! You will also become more interesting because you are truly interested in others and learning. Let this formula underlie all you do:

### *Knowledge + Planning x Action = Success*

Start challenging yourself. Start asking more questions. It's the difference between knowing and doing. Get into that place, get into that action. Don't think: *"Well, this doesn't really apply to me. I know it doesn't apply to me. You don't understand my business, it's different"*. Instead say, "How <u>could</u> this apply?" Once you take on that attitude, you'll see a change that could impact your business and your ideas, as well as your personal and professional development. We see this every day in the changes exhibited in our clients and their results.

## PERCEPTION

Perception is a critical part of your attitude. It is your ability to uncover solutions from challenges going on around you. Most innovations and discoveries actually came from that process.

# OMG! What's The Focus?

There has been a lot of great psychological study done about perception. One popular awareness test that used a video of passing basketballs can be found on YouTube and is called the "Selective Attention Test" by Daniel Simons. Notice how when you are focused on certain things, you can easily miss (or fail to perceive) when something else important is happening. This study is a great example of what we miss in our day-to-day lives. Whether or not you watch the YouTube video, here's another quick exercise to make the point clearer: Close your eyes right now and focus on the color red. Say to yourself "red" five times. Now open your eyes and look around the room – I'll bet you're noticing a lot more red objects or items containing red.

When we're looking for something in particular our perception shifts. If you focus on your problems or challenges, you will find more problems and challenges. Over time, you become a great problem finder and you perceive that your role is to find and fix problems. (At this point, you might as well buy yourself a cape to wear around the office.) You end up with a set of perceptions (beliefs) that are not particularly helpful - like all salesman are sleazy, no one pays their bills on time, or people never call back when they say they will. Your perception is 100% focused on the challenge and you will continue to find more of the same. For most of us, it's also true that once we establish our beliefs about someone or something, we only "see" (perceive) those things that support our beliefs -- and that can become a vicious cycle. What if you consciously worked on changing your perception to a positive, action-oriented paradigm? How can I take these challenges and create a solution? What can I do to attract people that can pay their bills? What are the attributes of an ideal salesman – the kind of sales person I would want to be? What could I do to improve my communications skills so I get calls returned more frequently?

Every invention has been created in response to challenges and obstacles. What once seemed impossible – like Bill Gates 1980 vision "a computer on every desk and in every home" – is now a computer on every person as our world becomes more and more mobile. Every time we needed to save money, or time, or when we needed to become more efficient, our solutions have come from answers to challenges solved by others. How can I solve this? What's a way around this? Look at challenges as exciting opportunities to create the next new solution or result.

One way to change your perception is to write a gratitude list. Sit with a clean sheet of paper and fill it with lists of all of the things that you are grateful for in your life. When you write one, you begin to notice and really appreciate what you have. Post the list where you will see it regularly or when you notice you're feeling down and review your list regularly. It's not possible to be negative and grateful at the same time. Try it! One of our executive clients has a series of family pictures (mostly of fun times with his kids) that he looks at first thing each morning (and if he needs a little boost during his day.) It's his "visual gratitude list".

Tom Rath, author of *How Full Is Your Bucket?*, uses the metaphor of the invisible bucket. His insights are based on rigorous research of human behavior and response. Metaphorically, everyone starts their day with a bucket of positive emotional energy and a dipper. Every day, we have over 20,000 interactions with others – an opportunity to effect someone's bucket. When we add to their bucket with our dipper by smiling, and/or giving them some form of a positive comment, we help fill their bucket (and ours as well). However, when we take away from their bucket with our scooper by our actions or negative responses or comments, we also diminish our own buckets of positive energy. So find reasons to compliment someone or share a smile. Help them with a challenge they were working on and these simple acts of kindness will add to your bucket as well, positively affecting your performance and well-being.

There is an area in our brains that serves an important function called Reticular Activating System, which we fondly refer to as the "RAS" for short. Your RAS serves as a filtration system to help you find whatever you are looking for. It's like a spam filter that determines what our conscious brain will notice. The RAS is located in our brain stem and functions to filter out stimuli so only certain images, smells, tastes, sensations, etc. are noticed and considered in our conscious minds. For example, how is your left foot feeling right now? Your brain is receiving signals at all times about the status of all parts of your body, but you were unlikely consciously noticing your left foot until you read that question. That's your RAS, filtering and presenting to your conscious mind what it asks for.

Have you ever bought a new car, then noticed that exact same car everywhere? That's your RAS. When you got that new car, your RAS filter turned on, allowing that stimuli to come into your consciousness. Every day you pass hundreds of cars but you only notice a small number of them–those that you have made important in some way. You're more likely to find something if you are specifically looking for it. This is why we recommend having specific goals, in writing that you review daily. You are regularly "setting your RAS" to find (and bring to your attention) those things in your environment that relate to those goals. As a result, you'll increase your chances of succeeding dramatically. You will identify opportunities for improvement and be able to take action.

Steven R. Covey's book, *Seven Habits of Highly Effective People,* is a great resource for personal development. We recommend it to everyone, and if you have not read it in a while, read it again. The number one habit Covey identifies in the book is Be Proactive. Covey describes it as "a pause button between stimulus and response - a button you can engage to pause and think about what is the principle-based response to your given situation." In other words, identify what you can do, what you can actively accomplish, and do it. Proactive people recognize, as Covey says, that they have "response-ability" – we all have the ability to choose our response to events that occur in our lives. Highly effective people are proactive and focus on the things they can actually influence.

# E + R = O

Events (E) are the moments throughout our day for which we do not plan. We have an idea what our day will be like when we wake up in the morning, but then the unexpected happens. Our response (R) to that event determines the outcome (O). We have no control over events, but we have 100% control over our response. Oftentimes we do not think that way. When someone yells at you, you yell back. Reality is, it was our choice to yell. Take control. Become more thoughtful, more mindful, more strategic. Push for responses that help you achieve your outcome. You get to choose! As Jim Rohn says: "It is not what happens that determines the major part of your future. What happens, happens to us all. It is what you do about what happens that counts."

So how do we improve our ability to choose better, more effective responses? Another great concept that our clients say has made the biggest difference in their lives and business is called "Above The Line".

Imagine a line like the wooden chair rail around your dining room. The line is like a "line of control". Below the line responses to things that happen keep us immobile and less likely to move forward productively. Below the line is **B**lame, **E**xcuses and **D**enial, which forms the acronym BED. You can choose to live below or above the line. When you live below the line, you blame other people, come up with excuses, and/or live in denial thinking "Everything's fine the way it is." Denial itself is another acronym which stands for "**D**idn't **E**ven **N**otice **I A**m **L**ying" – and who are we lying to? Ourselves. What is your Blame, Excuse, Denial? What is your BED? We all know the feeling of laying sick in bed, stagnating. You're not proactive, you're not moving forward. Stuck, with only reasons for not achieving results.

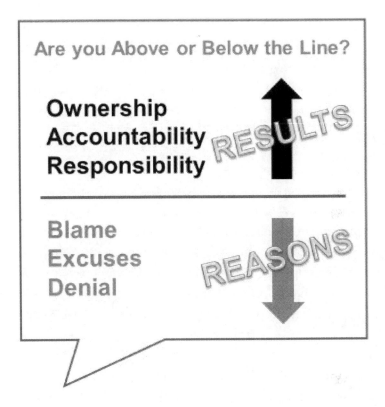

Now venture above the line, utilizing **O**wnership, **A**ccountability, and **R**esponsibility – which forms the acronym OAR. Once you take personal ownership, accountability of the facts and figures and responsibility for your response to everything that happens in your life, you have the control to steer the ship back into forward motion towards outcomes and results.

*"The greatest day in your life and mine is when we take total responsibility for our attitudes. That's the day we truly grow up."* **- John C. Maxwell**

Have you ever been "overwhelmed"? Or use the excuse of "I just didn't have enough time"? Is that above or below the line? The reality is we all have exactly the same amount of time (24 hours per day), but clearly some of us are better at managing that time than others. What if you attacked that reason with what you could do differently? Asking for example, What is something I can do to work on better investing my time, and how can I organize myself? What is one thing that I can do right now to change my circumstance? And if you begin to take accountability for implementing the changes necessary, then you will receive more discretionary time. That's you claiming responsibility. Becoming more accountable will actually drive results.

Ask any great sales person—they have quotas, they are held accountable and measured. They know whether they're making money or not. Finally, there's Ownership. Some days, you just need to own your ship and move forward. Instead of focusing on the problems, focus on how you will take them on. That is Ownership. Get back Above the Line to steer the ship!  The insight is this:  there are only two things in life – you either get results or you have your reasons. Success in business and in life is a result of consistently choosing RESULTS. One great book about management techniques is  called *It's Your Ship* by Captain D. Michael Abrashoff.  Captain Abrashoff, in his very first command, famously led a US Navy missile cruiser from worst to best performer in the Navy by empowering his team to take ownership for their results and be response-able.  Talk about OAR!

# FUN

Fun is something you can access at any moment. If you've ever been a person having fun or been around someone having fun, you can relate to what you see. Things are happening faster, the day goes by faster, you're more attracted to that person, you want to be around them, there's a smile on their face, there's energy, there's motion going on. These are all things we know are related to fun, yet we don't always access it. Business can be so challenging, so stressful, that it's easy to go to that "serious" place naturally –no smiling allowed when we're addressing challenges.  Do you really believe that?  Just realizing that fun is an advantage, it will speed up your day, it will attract people, but you have to actually make it happen. So what if you said "What is fun?" Make a list of it, make it part of your day, make it part of your team's day, and share it all around so you can have faster, more effective days. "If it isn't fun, it won't get done." (Or it certainly won't get done as fast or as effectively.)

# CHAPTER 1
## KEY THOUGHTS

- 3 Types of Focus
- Iceberg – **IVVM exercise**
- Be x Do = Have
- Perception/RAS – **Gratitude exercise**
- Above the Line

## OMG! WHAT'S THE FOCUS?
### ACTION STEPS

1) _____
2) _____
3) _____
4) _____
5) _____

## CONTINUED THINKING

- Focus - Goleman
- How Full is Your Bucket - Rath
- Five Major Pieces to the Life Puzzle - Rohn
- 7 Habits of Highly Effective People - Covey
- It's Your Ship – Captain Abrashoff

# 2

## Six Steps

*"To achieve great things, to grow a great business ... you have to think and plan long term ... short term thinking only produces short term results"* – **Brad Sugars**

The six steps are about achieving a true business. A lot of people claim to have a business. But if you leave on a cruise trip for a month and the business cannot run without you, then you really don't have a business. You have a very high risk job.

Maybe you love your high risk job, but JOB is just an acronym for:

**J**ust

**O**ver

**B**roke

If this is your current situation, you are supporting the business vs. the business supporting you.  As soon as you notice this, you have a great opportunity to take responsibility and push yourself toward building a real business. Often times business owners invest their entire lives into their business. They're shocked when they realize they have no saleable value in the business when the time comes for transition – and it WILL come. Focus on how you can make a business that could work without you. Build your business so that you do have retirement funds when it is time. Our definition of a "real business" is a "Commercial, profitable, saleable enterprise that <u>could</u> work without you (the owner)." Your business can only be as strong as its foundation. When you have a house, it is easy to build additions and expand on the already existing structure as long as the foundation can accommodate it. But if you decide to begin building additional floors in the future, you cannot do so without a change to the foundation—so it is important to make sure it is steady, strong, and durable.

Like building a foundation of a house, there are six essential steps of building a foundation for your business that will allow it to work effectively and profitably without you. Often times, our clients need to go back and shore-up the foundation of their businesses because they either did not know what to do in the beginning or they never expected to have the growth they achieved in their business.  When a business grows,  the systems and plans can become ineffective to run the current business effectively. We have seen this in all sizes of businesses and also those in business over 15 years or more. The "tools" are the same and have been proven around the world in over 1000 offices in over 50 countries. You should plan your foundation like you would a house -

taking into consideration the professionals that are involved such as the builder, the architect, the local governmental laws, the correct legal paperwork, understanding the budget, having the funding ahead of time, knowing how long the building will take, and, lastly, what the building plan looks like.

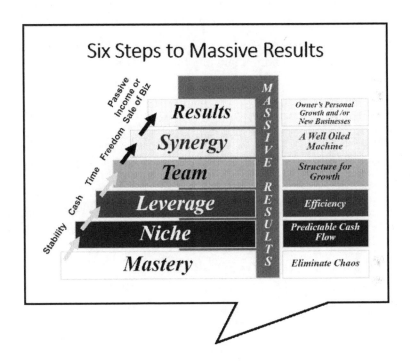

## STEP 1: MASTERY

The first step is laying down the Mastery level to eliminate chaos from the business. There are four parts: destination, delivery, financial, and self/time-management. The key thing we first work on are the financials. Many business owners we meet don't understand their financials to the level necessary for growth and success. Getting accurate, timely, and accrual based reports is critical for achieving a real business. The owner needs to receive the information necessary to make great strategic decisions and tactical, course altering decisions as well. We will discuss more on Financial Mastery in chapter 4 "Financials".

Let's focus next on destination mastery. If you don't know where you're going, or where you are now, it is impossible to create an effective plan. We have clients look forward to where they choose to be in three to five years. They visualize that as if it were today. If a local business writer were writing an article about your business at that future time, what would be the main points of the story. They visualize to really grasp how they can change to get to that vision. We'll explore this further later in this chapter when we discuss vision, mission, and culture.

Next, at the Mastery level, we also need to focus on "delivery mastery". Before we can begin working on building growth, we need to make sure you can consistently deliver your product or service. Are your systems for 'delivery' scalable? Are your processes documented and is there a plan for delivering at a point of higher demand? In other words – if your volume were to increase by 30%, what steps would you need to take to be certain the quality and consistency of your delivery is maintained.

Finally, at the foundational, mastery level is "Time Mastery". In reality, it's not really about managing time because time cannot be managed- it's about self-management related to how you invest your time. As the business owner, where you choose to focus your personal energy and time will make all the difference in your success.

## STEP 2: NICHE

The next place to evaluate is Niche. ActionCOACH's definition of Niche is no price competition. What is your unique Niche in the marketplace? What are guarantees you could put on that uniqueness?

This step is also where you start creating predictable cash flow. We will discuss more on Niche in chapter 5 "Marketing".

## STEP 3: LEVERAGE

The third step of laying your foundation is becoming more efficient through Leverage. For example, writing systems to standardize all aspects of your business and putting quality tracking and reporting procedures in place. We work with businesses to create more time and efficiency in the business. If you don't write it down you are forever destined to do it (yourself) over and over again! We discuss more on Leverage in chapter 4 "Financials" and chapter 7 "Systems".

## STEP 4: TEAM

Next step is developing your winning Team to structure the business for growth. How do you get new employees? How do you recruit them? How do you engage them? How are you as a leader? How do you make a more proactive team so they can support the business while you focus on your role as an owner? With a team comes the opportunity for freedom but only if you recruit, select, train and motivate effectively. You will learn more on this subject in chapter 8 "Team".

## STEP 5: SYNERGY

The fifth step is establishing Synergy. Synergy is about integrating the elements of mastery, niche, leverage and team to work together so that the whole result is greater than the simple sum of its parts. Now it is time to hire a general manager to manage on a day to day basis. The business really starts working like a well-oiled machine producing cash and freedom for the owner - you!

# STEP 6: RESULTS

The last step is the Results level. Now you've got a business. A commercially profitable, saleable enterprise that can work without you. What's next? Franchising? Licensing? Acquisition? Are you creating a new like-minded business, complementary to your own? Maybe you can learn a whole other skill, like real estate investing, business investing, stock market investing. At the results level, you are not the plumber, the pharmacist, or the lawyer anymore. You are a business owner. How are you going to challenge yourself in a new way?

**FREE RESOURCE DOWNLOAD**
6 Steps Mastery Checklist Tool
www.actioncoachtampabay.com/six

# REALITY CHECK

For most of you reading this book and especially for those who download and complete the *6 Steps Mastery Checklist Tool* (which we highly recommend), you will discover that you do not currently have many of these essential business practices in place. We personally have had hundreds of business owners in our market (and tens of thousands across the world) complete the Mastery Checklist. For the vast majority of owners, it's a real gut-check because they've had to answer "No" to most of the detailed questions about documentation or consistency of current business practices in the six steps. The first thing to remember is those type of results are normal even for very experienced (and large) businesses. One of the largest clients we coached, were in business for over 30 years with sales of nearly $1 Billion/year and the results of the checklist in many areas were about the same as everyone else. So if you have a lot of "No's", be grateful, this is a huge opportunity for you!

Just for a moment, pause and consider the performance and value of your company when you can finally answer "yes" to the vast majority of the questions across the six steps. Most of your competitors don't have this information or insights and if you engage an ActionCOACH, you can get the coaching help, experience and detailed systems to really accelerate the process. Recently, one of our clients successfully completed the sale of their business to a venture capital firm that is investing the capital to use their "proven business systems" to expand their former company statewide. Incidentally, that purchase deal was put together and facilitated by one of our other clients – a mergers and acquisitions firm. Even though the owners of that company had been in business for over 20 years, when we first met them they had no systems, no marketing plan and were working 7 days/week. If someone called off sick in "the plant", they had to fill in. They hadn't taken a vacation in 5 years. I remember their Mastery Checklist was filled with "no's". Within 12 months, they were growing, acquiring other underperforming businesses in their category and were able to take about 6 weeks of vacation time. Within another 18 months, they had nearly doubled in size and had begun the process of being acquired, in stages by a venture capital firm. The venture capital firm wanted two things, their growing cash flow and their comprehensive business systems. Our former clients are financially set for life and local business heroes  because of their community involvement and philanthropic endeavors. There is no reason your story couldn't be similar to theirs!

## KNOCKING DOWN BRICK WALLS

Most of us had dreams when we were kids. Dreams about who we wanted to be when we grew up like an artist, a firefighter, an astronaut, a doctor, or a nurse. Maybe you were like Randy Pausch, author of *The Last Lecture,* who wanted to be an imagineer at Disneyland. He applied to Disney multiple times and was rejected (nicely) each and every time but he never gave up on his dream.  Years later, when he developed some very specific and unique capabilities in virtual reality simulations while working at Carnegie Mellon University, Disney *approached him* and he had the opportunity to work on the Aladdin's Magic Carpet Ride attraction.  Unfortunately, as we grow a little older, people around us (with good intentions) tell us what is or isn't a realistic dream. Before we head toward our dreams, we stop. We go elsewhere. We're told: "You can't make money doing that" or "that's not realistic". Our dreams can become so compromised at a young age that we stop dreaming altogether.

Strengthen that resolve. Your dream/vision muscles might be a little weak and atrophied. Start exercising those muscles. Commit to get better at envisioning and pursuing your dreams. Make it easy for yourself. Put those dreams into visuals. Some of our clients have placed images of their dreams on their computer screen, some on their phones, some on their wall. Make it easy to look at them every day as it can be very powerful.

**FREE RESOURCE DOWNLOAD**

Dream Builder Exercise
www.actioncoachtampabay.com/dream

Randy Pausch (mentioned earlier) was a tenured professor at Carnegie Mellon University (CMU). At CMU, they have an academic tradition – each year a professor is challenged to speak to students as though hypothetically, this was their last lecture. Dr. Pauch's rendition of this traditional lecture went viral on the internet because for him, it wasn't hypothetical, he was dying of pancreatic cancer. He refers to something he called "the brick walls". Throughout life you're going to have brick walls–seemingly impenetrable obstacles to your dreams and goals. These walls are continuously in your face attempting to keep you out like the rejection letters Pausch received over and over from Disney. Pausch points out that brick walls are not there to keep you out, they're there to *challenge* you – to see how badly you want it. When you're more focused, more driven, and if you really want it – the brick walls will not stop you. Think about it. Every great American success story of exceptional accomplishment began this way – Thomas Edison, Henry Ford, Dr. Martin Luther King, Steve Jobs, Michael Jordan, even Walt Disney himself had multiple failed businesses and was fired by a newspaper editor because "he lacked imagination and had no good ideas".

## MISSION – VISION – VALUES (CULTURE) STATEMENTS

Jim Collins has written a number of books on top performing companies. He and his team of researchers looked at the common characteristics of the most successful companies vs. comparison companies who were in similar markets and circumstances. Universally, the main commonality was top performing companies have a very clear vision. In his first book, *Built to Last*, he gave these company's big goals a term - BHAGs. These BHAGs become the driving force for the vision.

**B**ig

**H**airy

**A**udacious

**G**oals

What is your company's vision statement? Get it out—not the kind that goes into a book some place and stays on the shelf, but rather the kind you talk about constantly and look at every day. The best vision statements create an expectation for the future state of your business. In five to ten years, how would you describe your business now? What would people say about your business? What are the key attributes of your business? An analogy of a business or personal vision is to imagine that you are at the base of a mountain looking up. Envision what it will look like when you reach the top of a mountain looking out across to other mountain tops miles away. You have an idea (a vision) for reaching the mountain top but the "way" or plan is not clear at the moment. Your idea for what it looks like or what you have accomplished when you arrive at the summit – that's a "Vision".

What's your company's mission statement? Your mission is how

you are going to actualize your vision. The mission is going to give you the "path" with milestones along the way that you can measure your progress of getting there by way of the mission towards your vision. In the analogy of the vision to reach the mountain top, your mission might include the use of new climbing gear or compass technology, an easier yet longer path and specific rest camps along the way.

When Microsoft was first created in 1975, their vision was to put a computer on every desk and in every home – and they weren't even a computer company. When they wrote that vision, it was a BHAG – a giant pipe dream that no one thought was possible. Now looking back, that vision seems small and simple as each of us has multiple computers at our office and home. That vision was achieved by a mission that partly focused on creating an operating system – Windows – that would make using computers easy and effective for everyone. When Bill Gates left the position of CEO at Microsoft in 2008, they developed a new vision for the company because they already achieved the original one.

The last part to achieving your vision's destination is to create the Value (or culture) words that will drive the behaviors necessary to achieve it. In the vision analogy of reaching the mountain peak, you might ask yourself – who will you need on your climbing team? What qualities and values will be important? What will they want you to provide? Similarly ask yourself with your vision in mind - What are your company's values? What values are important to the customer? To you? To your team? What values are important for the company to succeed? As you ponder the answer to each of the above questions, you'll notice that many of the words you choose will be the same or will overlap in meaning. We recommend you choose five to six words that resonate the most with you and your team. We recommend five to six because they will be more easily displayed, remembered and recited.

For example, our Vision at ActionCOACH Tampa Bay is to accelerate the economic growth of our community through business re-education and to be recognized as the leader in Helping Business Owners to Build a Saleable Business that Works Without Them. Our Mission at ActionCOACH Tampa Bay is to implement comprehensive business coaching and training systems that create accountability for our clients to achieve their goals and dreams in business and life. In 2007 when we founded our company, each of us picked two words that became our commitment as a team. During our first planning session, we all agreed to our values of Passion, Fun, Communication, Respect, Ownership and Integrity forming the acronym PFC-ROI to help aid in remembering them. We refer to these in all aspects of our business when selecting clients to work with, vendors to do business with, people in our lives, and the decisions that we make. We ask ourselves: "Is it consistent with our values?" We continue to strive to be congruent with our values and transparent in all of our dealings.

**FREE RESOURCE DOWNLOAD**

Vision – Mission – Culture Exercise
www.actioncoachtampabay.com/vmc

## ALL REAL PROGRESS STARTS WITH A PLAN

*"If we could first know where we are, and whither we are tending, we could better judge what to do, and how to do it."* - **Abraham Lincoln**

Our complete, one-page planning system is reviewed in detail in chapter 9 "Planning". We're bringing this to your attention now so as you read through the book, you can flag items or take some notes of sections that contain specific ideas that you know you'll want to begin working on right away. As an alternative, you may benefit from reading chapter 9 now (so you can "begin with the end in mind") and then review it again as you begin putting your plan together at the end of the book. Also you can use the provided end of chapter summaries to take notes on what five action steps you plan to implement out of each chapter. Those end of chapter action steps will be a great asset to you as you embark on chapter 9 and the task of building of your one-page, highly focused action plan.

## CHAPTER 2
### KEY THOUGHTS

◎ 4 Areas of Mastery
◎ 6 Steps to Building a Commercial, Profitable, Saleable Enterprise that Works Without You
◎ Brick Walls
◎ Vision – Mission – Culture

### OMG! WHAT'S THE FOCUS?
### ACTION STEPS

1) _____
2) _____
3) _____
4) _____
5) _____

### CONTINUED THINKING

◎ The Business Coach - Sugars
◎ Built to Last - Collins
◎ The Last Lecture - Pausch
◎ The Answer – Assaraf & Smith
◎ Start with Why - Sinek

# 3

# Productivity

*"Being busy does not always mean real work. The object of all work is production or accomplishment and to either of these ends there must be forethought, system, planning, intelligence, and honest purpose, as well as perspiration. Seeming to do is not doing."* - **Thomas A. Edison**

We are all created equal in the way that everybody starts the day with 24 hours and has until the end of the day to invest them wisely before they expire. Unlike money, where you can gain it back, once time is gone, your time is gone. There's no recouping time. Productivity is about effectively using your time to get a meaningful return.

People perceive time differently. In his book *The Cashflow Quadrant,* Robert Kiyosaki explains the difference between the business mindset and the employee/self-employed mindset. Are you on the employee side or the business owner/investor (entrepreneurial) side of the quadrant?

Maybe you don't realize there is a choice. Under an employee's mentality, you get paid a certain amount for every hour you work. You have to fill in the gap on those forty hour work weeks. With an entrepreneurial mentality, you're constantly thinking about returns on your investment in time. As an owner you don't think, "How can I fill a forty-hour work week?" You think, "How can I get a forty-hour work week done in only three days? In two days? In one? In 4 hours? Who can I get to operate my system so I don't have to be here at all?" Then you use the rest of that week to produce something for the future to work ON the business verses IN the business. An example might be researching a new idea to invest in or negotiating the next merger or acquisition.

As an employee, earning $1,000 per hour is unlikely but as an entrepreneur you can make more per hour than you'd ever thought possible. You have to go from an *earning* money mentality to a *making* money mentality.

## ENTREPRENEURIAL LADDER

If you want to be on the entrepreneurial side, understand where you lie on the entrepreneurial ladder and what rung you need to learn next to more forward towards unlimited money making possibilities. Each rung you climb presents a new challenge, new focus and a new mentality.

## STUDENT

The ladder starts at the bottom rung, with our first job - being a student. As a student, we spend time and money with the hopes of getting a larger return for our investment. At this phase, we are not earning anything – we are costing money and sometimes incurring debt.

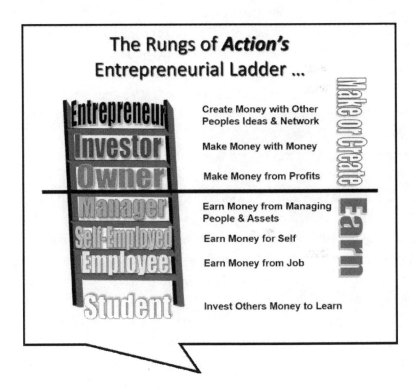

## EMPLOYEE

At some point, we get a job, become an employee. As an employee, we have a set schedule of time for a certain amount of money back per hour. At this rung your earnings are limited to the number of hours you clock-in for and the rate of value per hour your company or position assigns to you. Therefore, the busier you are – the more hours and overtime hours you work – the more you earn. Many people stay at this level all their lives. But if you are inclined to make more money, to gain more freedom, perhaps you should climb to the next rung—self-employment.

## SELF-EMPLOYED

Now you are self-employed. You are your own boss. Therefore, you're responsible for every task of the business. As an employee, you are not cognitive of the activities happening around you like marketing, admin, bookkeeping, customer service, invoicing, sales, financials, planning and systems development. Under self-employment, you have to become aware because what was once an entire department is now a department of one - you. *If I don't follow up on these leads, there's no money. If I don't service my clients correctly, I could have returns and problems with my reputation and repeat business. If I don't market consistently, I'm running out of leads.* Now you are more aware of how you spend your time and how well you are balancing these other roles you have taken on. It is often described as a seesaw going back and forth from marketing to get new business to delivering the product or service to the customer. The major challenge of this rung is continuing to view time the same way you did when you were an employee. Self-employment has no guaranteed salary based on busyness – you must now go get the money you earn. That means if you spend too much time doing non-revenue generating activity – your earnings could be zero even after working a forty-hour work week (or more).

## MANAGER

After self-employment, you can climb up to a manager. You're an all-star now. You're capped out on time, so you decide to hire some people. This is an interesting transition. Not only is your time spent differently, now your time involves another element: the team. The challenge here is managing them to be all-stars and you step down from the top performer role. Sharing experience with your new team members so they can outperform you. They will need a lot of teaching and mentoring. Many businesses fail here because the owners act like they're still self-employed. When it was just you – you did everything, you did it your way, and you proved you were the best at doing it. However, there comes a point when even the most type A, super human, over-achiever taps out on 24 hours per day time limit. The only way to get to the next level of productivity is to increase your daily time limit by hiring more people. Are you thinking about recruiting, onboarding and training so you have more time to manage the business? As a manager, the amount you earn depends on your ability to stop doing it all and start managing your team to do it for you leveraging everything you learned thus far.

# OWNER

At the next level, you become an owner. This is where the machine is really running. Your business is working without you. A manager is on board running it. Now you're getting a profit return on your investment. You are more *focused* on working ON the business, pulling yourself out of your previous roles and focusing your time solely on where you can invest to achieve more profitability. This is where the habits you formed earlier come into play as you *focus* on the growth of the business. The business cycle is working smoothly - you support the team, the team supports the customers, the customers support the business, and the business supports the owner with profits. You finally make the shift from earning money to making money in the form of profit.

# INVESTOR

Your business is working for you. You're getting residual income and the business is kicking off more cash than you've ever seen in your life. But how do you become an investor? How do you take money earned and reinvest it to double, triple, quadruple the money back? Here you learn investing in other businesses, real estate and/or stocks or managing investment portfolios. And once you learn investing, everything compounds to your benefit. You are making money with money.

## ENTREPRENEURIAL LEVEL

Final rung, top of the ladder, is the entrepreneurial level. You've proven yourself. You can produce money from a business, reinvest it, and get it back over and over again. Now other people come to you saying, "here's my money, make something of it, please" or "here's my idea please turn it into money". Now, you're creating money with other people's money, ideas and network - and you most likely have multiple business interests that return re-occurring profit to you!

## ROI ON TIME

A lot of business owners feel challenged.  They ask, "When do I move from self-employed to manager? When should I hire my first team member?" Usually, these questions remain unanswered for far too long. Many continue working without realizing the options available for leveraging time.

You don't have to employ a full-time professional, or even someone at a low skill level. There are tons of options starting out. Virtual assistant services and interns for example. Online, there's a lot of inexpensive companies, freelancers, apps, and free technology you can leverage. Realize what's taking up most of your time. Realize that without hired help, YOUR unique talent and best opportunity for return on YOUR time could be wasted.  As Brad Sugars, founder of ActionCOACH says,  "The wage you save could be costing you a fortune." In order to get a return on your time, you have to measure it.

Keep a ROI (Return On Investment) of your time diary – which is a log of your time each day so you know where it is going and can build a plan to become more effective. You'll start seeing, not only where your time is going, but where it fits in different brackets: high skill or low skill, expense or income, high fun or low fun. Look at your schedule. What do you love to do versus what you hate to do? If you don't love the work, it's probably not getting done. And if it is, it's not being done very well. How much longer can your business survive with the lackluster effort? If you didn't know the owner, would you still be employed doing that work for the company? Why not hire someone who would actually enjoy the work that you hate?

Stephen Covey, again, author of *Seven Habits of Highly Effective People,* developed a great model for where we spend our time (See Time Quadrants illustration on next page.) In the upper left-hand corner, quadrant one, are those things that are important and urgent, such as client calls, things you need to tend to right away. Sometimes it's family oriented, like picking up your daughter from school because she is not feeling well. Sometimes, there are ways those urgent matters could be reduced.

On the upper right-hand corner is quadrant two. These are activities which are important, but not urgent. Some examples might include: research and planning, developing systems for your business, and writing new marketing plans and new organizational structures. Working to improve or deepen important relationships and reading for personal development are other examples. These are important for your business. But are they urgent? Do people call saying, "Hey, work on your plan for next year. You know it's urgent. You need to read that book right now"? No! No one says that. But you'll find that with a little planning and system developing, you can actually reduce the time you are spending in the other quadrants that are taking over your life. *Focus* and invest more time in quadrant two. How do we redirect our time to quadrant two? *Allocate.*

Quadrant three is in the bottom left-hand side. These are urgent activities that are not important. For example, your phone rings and declares itself as an urgent matter, so you answer it immediately. But frequently, those phone calls are not important. Most emails belong in quadrant three. By stopping or even reducing the time spend constantly checking and responding to new emails, you can spend more time working on those things that are important but not urgent.

We had a client who built his business and sold it to a large, international IT consulting company. The client literally turned off his email from his cell phone, so he could only look at it certain times every day. Being in the IT industry, his team thought the idea of limiting access to technology was crazy. However, he realized that he needed to build a small barrier to stop the habit of urgently checking his email so that the time he was wasting could be reallocated to quadrant two tasks with a higher importance and return. Eventually, this same IT consulting company also changed their policy about meetings, reducing them from an hour to 45 minutes. What can you do to reallocate more time to quadrant two tasks?

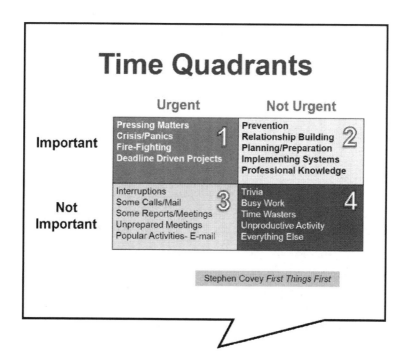

Quadrant four, bottom right-hand side. Not urgent and not important. Timewasters. How much time do you spend watching TV? Maybe you're a sports fan. How many hours do you listen to sports talk radio? Is that really helping your business? Your life? Is it imperative that you play those video games right now?

Now that you've identified what's in the two "not important" quadrants three and four, consider how you could reallocate at least some of the time consumed by those activities into quadrant two. That's how you advance both life and business.

## ENTERTAINMENT VS EDUCATION

Darren Hardy, author of *The Compound Effect,* talks about the impact that small changes or decisions repeated consistently (habits) can compound and have a huge impact on our results in business and in life in the long run. If you come from a small community in Western Pennsylvania, you probably grew up with the belief that manual labor and having a job was what you did every day. That's how you produce results - in the fields, on the farms, tending to animals. Physical labor and hands on work was what produced results. Nowadays, results are less focused on the physical and more focused on the intellectual. America is a knowledge and skills based environment in which our ability to solve problems, communicate and motivate others is the basis for remuneration. The more we improve our brain, the more effective (and valuable) we become at our work. In the old days we sharpened our saws, or other tools of manual labor, today we sharpen our brains.

Darren Hardy, who has interviewed countless successful actors, entrepreneurs and self-made millionaires as the editor of *Success Magazine*, spoke to hundreds of coaches and business owners at ActionCOACH's annual Business Excellence Forum and Awards about the concept of the "E:E ratio". Hardy pointed out the amount of time (and money) adult Americans spend on entertainment versus education. According to Hardy, it's a staggering 90:10. That's 90% of discretionary time on entertainment to 10% spent on education. Imagine the results you would see in a year from now when you impact that ratio by replacing some of your entertainment time with education.

People claim they don't have time to read, to study, to even attend workshops and seminars. But step back and look at your discretionary time. If you move some of that entertainment time to "tune-up" time by improving your education, business insight and personal performance, you'll discover a tremendous impact on the quality of your life.

Here's a story to illustrate this point: A professor walks into a college class carrying a clear glass bucket. Inside there are large rocks. "Is the bucket full?" he asks the students. They say "yes". The professor pulls out a bag of pebbles, dumps them inside, and shakes the bucket. "Is it full now?" Some say "yes", some say "no".

The professor pours a bag of sand into the bucket. "How about now?" They're catching on. "No", they say, "Not yet". Finally, the professor pours water into the bucket of rocks, pebbles and sand. Now the bucket is completely full.  So here's the insight:  if he hadn't put the big rocks in first, they would never have fit at the end - nor the pebbles before the sand nor the sand before the water.

Every day, week, month, etc. we start with a schedule – our calendar that is like an empty bucket. It's up to us to figure out what actually goes in AND in what order. The big rocks are the quadrant 2 activities – those things which are important but may not be urgent  - activities that will improve your business and life in the long run. But , instead, we allow the urgent small and many times unimportant things - the sand, pebbles and water to get in our schedules first.  Are you intentionally (or unintentionally) majoring in minor things? If you've been allowing urgent and unimportant things to fill your bucket first, then you probably feel like you never have enough time left over for reading, vacation, volunteering or *me* time.

Start a fresh, blank default calendar. Look at every week as an empty bucket. In a typical work week, place your big rocks in first. Then pour the rest of the sludge in. By pouring in the sludge after, you're allowing space in your week to accomplish that which is truly important. At the end of your life, will you likely reflect back and wish you had spent more time texting and emailing or will you wish you had spent more time with building important relationships, traveling and improving your knowledge and insights?

**FREE RESOURCE DOWNLOAD**

Default Calendar Tool
www.actioncoachtampabay.com/calendar

## DISTRACTIONS

Very few people can actually multitask. Your brain isn't built to do more than one thing at a time. When we think we're "multitasking" we're actually "switch tasking". Switching from one task to another task. Studies have demonstrated that this behavior causes up to a 40% loss in productivity! And over time, this can actually cause our brains to lose measurable ability to focus and concentrate. The good news is that if you stop this behavior now, your brain can fully recover over time. There are numerous strategies to reduce this hindrance on focus and productivity. We'll also give you a list of "10 Ways to Invest Time" at the end of this chapter. It's up to you to implement new habits and rituals, to create the environment for clear thinking and focus that can dramatically improve your business and your life.

Verne Harnish, mentor and writer of *Mastering the Rockefeller Habits,* among others, created his own ritual based on one of the practices of John D. Rockefeller (America's 1ˢᵗ Billionaire).  Every day you set a specific time to meet with your team for no more than 15 minutes to reset the focus and support for one another for the day. He calls this a "daily huddle". Your team discusses their top priorities for the day and where they may need help from you or someone else.  They should also discuss something positive that has happened or is working well. We find this method very helpful. Whether small or large, daily huddles will work to keep your team focused on the most important goals of the organization and ways to support one another.

Another wildly success strategy for creating productivity and focus: MI5, or Most Important 5. At the end of each day, write down the top five things you want to accomplish the next day. The act of writing it down really helps you get those goals done. You should be required to do it for your 90-day plan, because those goals drive your production, accelerating your business. Your daily activity should lead to your goals and will bring you massive results through consistency.

We teach our clients about another great productivity ritual based on a quote from Mark Twain.  Mark Twain reportedly said: "If you eat a frog for breakfast, nothing worse will happen to you the rest of the day." If you have a large project you want completed, do it first thing in the morning. Look at your MI5 list and pick the most important item on the list – do that first! Yes, even before looking at email. Our brains are at their most productive first thing in the morning and you'll have the highest level of energy to get it done. Many people respond to emails first thing in the morning. Emails are full of problems. Your brain's tied up in all these challenges. Instead, you could set aside time first thing and actually work on your most important task. Just think how that would feel. The impact for the rest of your day could be enormously positive.

If you have more than one frog, eat the ugliest one first. If you browse your frogs, you're probably not going to eat them as they stare at you. Be more proactive. Start munching away. Recently, one of our clients had a pile of papers on her desk. A big plastic frog sat on top, and when she was asked about them, she said, "That's my frog project for tomorrow morning." She had planned the night before what she would work on the very first thing next day. She was "setting the table" – great idea. But most importantly, it helped her productivity (and mood) increase dramatically.

**FREE RESOURCE DOWNLOAD**

Eat The Frog – MI5 Tool
www.actioncoachtampabay.com/frog

# 10 WAYS TO INVEST TIME

1. **Tame the phone and email**. Keep them in control, have a system that works around them. Have a gatekeeper who answers your calls. Forward phone messages to your email, so you can look at it at your leisure. Schedule only specific times during the day for email. Turn-off all email (and text) alerts. If it's truly an emergency – give trusted individuals an alternative method to reach you.

2. **Practice minimizing meetings.** Think about our client working with 45 minute meetings. Whoever said meetings had to last an hour? Most 30 minute meetings can be competed in half the time. Be fanatical about people being on time and have a tight agenda.

3. **Have an action plan and update it.** Make sure all activities are tied to an important goal or outcome. Once you do this on a

weekly and daily basis it will become one of your best habits. Just imagine if your entire company did it, what would be your results?

4. **Make and use lists.** Think of lists as storage containers outside of your brain. Think it once, write it down and you will have more room in your brain to process more important activities.

5. **Link actions to goals.** If your activities are not related to accomplishing your goals that you defined, refocus your activity and get back on plan. Consider developing a "To-Stop Doing List" for activities you are going to stop because they don't provide results or link to your goals.

6. **Default diary and scheduling.** We had a client one time working between two different locations. We coached her into visiting one location twice a week and the other three locations times a week. It minimized her travel time greatly. It's amazing what you can get done if you reschedule your default calendar.

7. **Daily planning ritual.** Control the bookends - the beginning and ends of your days. Again, eat that ugly frog early and first! Plan for tomorrow before you end your day.

8. **Keep a militant attitude.** If you do not protect or value your time, how can you expect anyone else to respect it? Eliminate "Got a minute?" meetings whenever possible.

9. **Mobile university:** Use your car and "odd lot-times" (waiting for an appointment, jogging etc.) to learn more. Audio books are a great option for this. Nourish your brain. Learn and apply new knowledge. Be inspired to change!

10. **Leverage, use it.** Look at all of your available resources and leverage them. Can you get someone to do your errands, house

cleaning, delivering your dry cleaning, mending your clothes or shopping for groceries so you can use your time at the highest and best value of your skill set? Figure it out...it's your life time that is ticking AWAY. Get *focused*!

## CHAPTER 3
## KEY THOUGHTS

◎ Return on Time Investment
◎ Entrepreneurial Ladder
◎ Entertainment vs. Education - E:E Ratio
◎ Default Calendar
◎ Eliminating Distractions
◎ Time Tips

## OMG! WHAT'S THE FOCUS?
## ACTION STEPS

1) _____
2) _____
3) _____
4) _____
5) _____

## CONTINUED
## THINKING

◎ Billionaire in Training - Sugars
◎ The Cashflow Quadrant- Kiyosaki
◎ 7 Habits of Highly Effective People - Covey
◎ Mastering the Rockefeller Habits – Harnish
◎ The Compounding Effect – Hardy

# 4

# Financials

*"Sadly, most businesses are struggling financially and they will stay that way because the owner is too busy operating and not running the business end of the business. It's not that they don't want to.... It's that no one ever taught them how. As Warren Buffett said, "If you can't read the scoreboard, you don't know the score. If you don't know the score, you can't tell the winners from the losers."*- **Keith J. Cunningham**

Financials are the language of business. If you can't speak (or understand) the basics of the language, you're going to have a hard time communicating with others in business or knowing what is going on around you. Your business financials are telling you about exciting opportunities and real dangers in the environment but if you don't understand what is being said, you have little chance of responding appropriately. A large number of business failures (>75%) fail in large part due to a lack of good financial planning and accurate *focus* on margins, cash flow, and real-time trends.

Perhaps a more useful metaphor is to think of business like a game – maybe one of the most important games in your life with real winners and unfortunately, real losers. The financial reports in a business provide you the score and the stats on all of your players and team's performance. If you don't know the score, you don't know if you're winning or losing. And if you don't keep stats on your players, you won't really know who is contributing and who is not and if they are improving over time or in a slump – needing some coaching or perhaps retirement.

Think of a time when you were watching a football game either on TV or in the stands. You don't reserve your cheers for only when your team crosses the goal line and scores, do you? And you certainly don't wait until days or weeks after the game to get a report telling you if your team won or lost. During the game, you cheer every time there's progress of your team towards the goal. Those funny lines (hash marks) on the field inform the crowd whether the team is progressing and moving forward or not. And you cheer the accomplishments of the offensive team as well as the defensive team and of course, the special teams. But you can only cheer if you know what's expected and how the team (or an individual) is doing against those expectations of good, superior or bad performance in "real-time". It's the same with business financials. Sure, there's a report showing the overall big score at the end (including some key stats). But you also need those lines and other indicators to know whether it's going well or not on a daily and weekly basis. If you determine you're losing ground, this allows you to decide if you should change the overall strategy, change some of the play calling (because they are not working) or remove some individual players due to poor execution or skill. But if you don't have any way to measure performance of key indicators during the game, how can you make the right coaching decisions?

## CASH-BASIS VS. ACCRUAL ACCOUNTING

Before you can start really understanding business transactions, you must decide to use accrual accounting vs. cash basis accounting. If you record your financial transactions using the accrual method, most accounting software programs (i.e. QuickBooks) will be able to provide cash-basis reports as well so you can look at it either way. BUT the opposite is not true - if you only record your transactions on a cash basis, your accounting software will not be able to produce accurate accrual method reports and you cannot fully evaluate your business performance in "real-time".

The key difference between these two accounting methods is in how you record your cash transactions. With cash basis accounting, you only record transactions in the books when cash actually changes hands, meaning when cash payment is received by the company from customers or paid out by the company for purchases or other services. "Cash payment" includes payments in the form of cash, check, credit card, electronic transfer, or other means except credit or "terms" extended by or to your business. Think for a moment about the implications on your ability to evaluate your business's current performance when there is no provision in the cash basis accounting method to record and track money due from customers at some time in the future. Likewise, there is no provision to record money you owe to a supplier/vendor that is due to be paid in the future even though you've already received (and maybe even resold) their goods or services.

Many small businesses are run by a sole proprietor or a small group of partners and use cash basis accounting because it's "easy". Since taxes are paid on a cash basis, it is the only type of reporting required by the government and the business' accountant hired to calculate the business and owner's tax obligations.

In our football metaphor, it would be like watching the game but certain types of plays from the team you are following are omitted from view and are not even reflected in the score or stats during the game. In fact, this continues all season. Now after the season is over, the plays and their implications on the season's overall record get added back into the results. Based on the games you watched all season, you thought you were winning but now you discover that you and your team must have lost a lot more games than you realized and the coach missed numerous opportunities to adjust the critical plays during the season. Oh well, there's always next year...

Cash basis accounting does a good job of tracking cash flow, but it does a poor job of matching revenues earned with money laid out for expenses. This deficiency is a problem particularly when, as it often happens, a company buys products in one month and sells those products in the next month or incurs the expense of providing products and/or services in one month but does not get paid for 30-45 days.

For example, you buy products in June with cash and incur outside labor expense to install the products for a customer. Total cost to you for products and labor is $2,000. Your customer pays your invoice in 30 days (the terms you established) so in July you receive the $2,500 cash for the sale. When you close the books at the end of June, you have recorded the $2,000 expense with no revenue to offset it. This scenario repeats multiple times each month. Your month-end report shows a $500 loss for June. In July, your month-end report shows a $2,500 profit. Was July really 4 times as profitable as June? What can we learn from the "loss" we experienced in June and what did we do differently to succeed in July? In actuality, you have no idea what your efforts produced in actual profit or loss for the business activity and sales in those two months so there are no real opportunities to make adjustments in strategy and execution.

# OMG! What's The Focus?

With accrual accounting, you record all transactions in the books when they occur, even if no cash changes hands. For example, if you sell on store credit, you record the transaction immediately as income and enter it into an Accounts Receivable (A/R) account until you receive payment. If you buy goods on credit, you immediately record it as an expanse and enter the transaction into an Accounts Payable (A/P) account until you pay out cash. The total A/R and A/P is reflected on your balance sheet as an asset and liability for future settlement and in the earlier example, June's results would have shown a $500 (expected) profit in the same month as your expense on the P&L report. Over time, this is the only way to see how you and your teams are performing and whether the business activity is successful or not.

Like cash basis accounting, accrual accounting can have its drawbacks if you don't understand the differences. It does a great job of matching revenues and expenses, but it does not reflect actual cash flows in and out. Because you record revenue when the transaction occurs and not when you collect the cash, your income (P&L) statement can look great even if you don't have cash in the bank. For example, suppose you're running a contracting company and completing jobs on a daily basis. You can record the revenue upon completion of the job even if you haven't yet collected the cash. If your customers are slow to pay, you may end up with lots of revenue but little cash. If you use the accrual accounting method, *which we highly recommend*, you must also monitor cash flow (preferably on a weekly basis) to be sure the business has enough cash on hand to operate the business. Also, if you record your transactions on an accrual basis, you can also get a cash basis report at any time with a few clicks.

> *Authors Note: As you read this section of the chapter on the Big Three Documents, have a copy of your financial reports handy so you can reference your actual reports as you read each section. Have these reports printed or prepared: Balance Sheet – most recent completed month-end & prior year-end; Income Statement (P&L) for the most recent completed period & prior year-end; and Cash Flow Statement for your most recent completed period. Also keep a pad of paper to document notes and questions for your coach or accountant. If for some reason,*

*you don't have access to these reports (or they're cash-basis only), go to this link on our website and download some simple examples to follow along.*

**FREE RESOURCE DOWNLOAD**

Big 3 Financial Documents Examples
www.actioncoachtampabay.com/three

# THE BIG THREE DOCUMENTS

To understand the financial performance of your business, there are three basic reports to understand: the Balance Sheet, the Profit and Loss (Income) Statement and the Cash Flow Report.

# #1 BALANCE SHEET

The first document is the balance sheet. It tells you the current status of your business, like a snapshot. It provides a picture of the financial health of a business at a given moment. The balance sheet is usually reviewed at the close of an accounting period (such as month end, quarterly and annual). It lists in detail those material and intangible items the business owns (known as its assets) and what money the business owes, either to its creditors (liabilities) or to its owners (shareholders' equity or net worth of the business). The insights that can be gleaned from a balance sheet are usually enhanced if the current report is compared to a prior period (such as prior year same period or year-end balance sheets).

Assets include not only cash, merchandise inventory, land, buildings, equipment, machinery, furniture, patents, trademarks, and the like, but also money due from individuals or other businesses (known as accounts receivable).

OMG! What's The Focus?

Liabilities are monies acquired for a business through loans or monies owed to others for products or services to the business on credit. Creditors do not acquire business ownership, but promissory notes to be paid at a designated future date.

Shareholders' equity (or net worth or capital or retained earnings) is money put into or left in a business by its owners for use by the business in acquiring assets.

At any given time, a business's assets equal the total contributions by the creditors and owners, as illustrated by the following formula for the Balance Sheet:

**Assets = Liabilities + Owners' Equity (Net worth)**

This formula is a basic premise of accounting. If a business owes more money to creditors than it possesses in value of assets owned, the net worth or owner's equity of the business will be a negative number.

The Balance Sheet is designed to show how the assets, liabilities, and net worth of a business are distributed at any given time. It is usually prepared at regular intervals e.g., at each month's end, but especially at the end of each fiscal (accounting) year.

By regularly preparing this summary of what the business owns and owes (the Balance Sheet), the business owner can identify and analyze trends in the financial strength of the business. It permits timely modifications, such as gradually decreasing the amount of money the business owes to creditors and increasing the amount the business owes its owners.

All Balance Sheets contain the same categories of assets, liabilities, and net worth. Assets are arranged in decreasing order of how quickly they can be turned into cash (liquidity). Liabilities are listed in order of how soon they must be repaid, followed by retained earnings (net worth or owner's equity). Assets and liabilities are broken down into specific categories as follows:

*Assets:* An asset is anything the business owns that has monetary value.

- <u>Current Assets</u> include cash, government securities, marketable securities, accounts receivable, notes receivable (other than from officers or employees), inventories, prepaid expenses, and any other item that could be converted into cash within one year in the normal course of business.

- <u>Fixed Assets</u> are those acquired for long-term use in a business such as land, plant, equipment, machinery, leasehold improvements, furniture, fixtures, and any other items with an expected useful business life measured in years (as opposed to items that will wear out or be used up in less than one year and are usually expensed when they are purchased). These assets are typically not for resale and are recorded in the Balance Sheet at their net cost less accumulated depreciation. (Depreciation is in some cases, strictly a mechanism for determining how much of a business related purchase may be applied as an expense each year for calculating profits and taxes owed. For example all real estate gets depreciated but has perpetual value and useful life.)

- <u>Other Assets</u> include intangible assets, such as patents, royalty arrangements, copyrights, exclusive use contracts, good will and notes receivable from officers and employees.

*Liabilities:* Liabilities are the claims of creditors against the assets of the business (debts owed by the business).

- <u>Current Liabilities</u> are accounts payable – A/P, notes payable to banks, accrued expenses (wages, salaries), taxes payable, the current portion (due within one year) of long-term debt, and other obligations to creditors due within one year.

- <u>Long-Term Liabilities</u> are mortgages, intermediate and long-term bank loans, equipment loans, and any other obligation for money due to a creditor with a maturity longer than one year.

*Net Worth* (sometimes labeled "retained earnings" or "owner's equity") are the assets of the business minus its liabilities. Net worth equals the owner's equity. This equity is the investment by the owner <u>plus</u> any profits or minus any losses that have accumulated in the business.

The categories and format of the Balance Sheet are established by a system known as Generally Accepted Accounting Principles (GAAP). The system is applied to all companies, large or small, so anyone reading the Balance Sheet can readily understand the story it tells.

**Assets = Liabilities + Net worth (owners' equity)**

# #2  PROFIT & LOSS (INCOME) STATEMENT

Second is the Profit & Loss statement or sometimes called an Income Statement or abbreviated as "P&L". The P&L is the most common report business owners look at. They look at the bottom right of the report - the net profit, to decide whether they're drinking in pain or in celebration. However, the net profit on the P&L is at least partially theoretical. You can actually spend cash in the bank but you can't spend net profit on the P&L. You may not have money in the bank, and yet the report might accurately indicate that your business is profitable. There are two parts to any transaction – the promise and the settlement and often they do not occur simultaneously.

The Statement of Income (P&L) is a measurement of a company's sales and expenses over a specific period of time. It is also prepared at regular intervals (again, each month and fiscal year end) to show the results of operating during those accounting periods. It too follows Generally Accepted Accounting Principles (GAAP) and contains specific revenue and expense categories regardless of the nature of the business.

The P&L statement gives you a number of important things to understand. The top starts with listing sources of revenue (income) often termed:

*Gross Revenue* (in QuickBooks – Income) shows how much money the business has generated from sales of products or service in that reporting period. Totaling all of the sources of gross revenue (income) gives you the "Top Line". In QuickBooks, it's termed "Total Income".

*Cost of Goods Sold* - The next items recorded on the P&L are the cost of material (and sometimes labor) that is directly attributable to the sales (income) listed above in that reporting period. This is the "Cost of Goods Sold" (COGS). If you're selling pens, for example and you sell each pen for $1.00 then your income (gross revenue) would be $500 if you sold 500 pens last period. The raw materials used to produce that pen, along with the portion of direct labor required to produce each pen is that pen's cost of goods sold (COGS). If the COGS for each pen was $0.40, your recorded COGS for the 500 pens sold on the P&L would be $200. When you subtract the COGS from the gross revenue (sales, income), you get what's called the Gross Profit (or Gross Margin). In the case of your pen sales, your Gross Profit (GP) would be $300 or 60% of total income (Gross Profit/Income).

Your gross profit dollar amount will likely be different month to month depending on the volume and types (mix) of products sold as well as variation in the cost of the materials. The best comparisons are in noticing your GP% (sometimes called your "margin") because that ratio of GP to Total Income should be relatively stable (or improving) independent of volume. You can compare adjacent periods and year over year to see your trends in GP earnings (what you get to keep) from sales. Obviously, if the business margins aren't stable or improving, the owner needs to understand it better and drill down to determine the drivers of the trends being observed. From the standpoint of potential impact, margin is one of the greatest opportunities for improvement in any business.

The gross profit is one of the most important and exciting indicators for business – we'll explain why at the end of this section. Gross Profit should be the primary focus for businesses looking to grow and achieve the next level of success. Gross profit must cover the next items listed on your P&L –

*Fixed Expenses* (or "Overhead" – termed "Total Expenses" in QuickBooks) are those expenses that regularly occur that are not directly tied to the sale of a product or service. These expenses include fixed (so called "Overhead") expenses i.e. salaries, wages, payroll taxes and benefits, rent, utilities, maintenance expenses, office supplies, internet expenses, postage, automobile/vehicle expenses, insurance, marketing – including entertainment expense, legal and accounting expenses as well as depreciation (sometimes not included until year-end).

*Net Operating Income (Profit)* – This is the net income generated as a result of the operating activities of the business before adjusting for non-operating income or expenses.

*Other Income* – This is income from activities other than normal business activities such as from investments, earned interest on customer charge accounts, rental income or perhaps profit from the sale of non-inventory assets – i.e. equipment or real estate.

*Other Expenses* – These are expenses from activities other than normal business activities such as from interest expense, write-off of a loss from investments or a law suit.

*Net Profit (or Loss) before Tax* (the figure on which your tax is calculated)

*Income Taxes* (if any are due)

*Net Profit (or Loss) After Tax* - YEAH! This is the capital generated by your business.

As promised earlier, here's why we say Gross Profit is the most important and exciting indicator for business. Once your Gross Profit is sufficient to pay your Fixed Expenses, every penny in excess Gross Profit creates your Net Operating Profit. Since Fixed Expenses are relatively "Fixed", as long as you manage your overhead expenses, all growth in Gross Profit results in more Net Profit! So a *Focus* on Gross Profit is a *focus* on winning the game of business! Once fully converted to cash (and adjusted by non-operating activity), that is what's termed "Free Cash Flow" – or the total cash (capital) available for the owner after all expenses (free of any encumbrances). That's also what creates true Freedom for the owner – now that's something on which to *FOCUS!*

# #3  CASH FLOW REPORT

Third is the cash flow report or "Statement of Cash Flows". This report shows the cash produced and used by your business within the reporting period (monthly, quarterly, annually). Cash flow is the very life blood of a business. If a small to medium sized company runs out of cash, it dies. The cash flow statement tells you whether the abstract profits recorded on the income (P&L) statement are being converted into cash in the bank. There are three types of activities that can produce, or reduce, cash in a business:

# OMG! What's The Focus?

*Operating Cash Flow (OCF)* - The top line of the cash flow statement is collections from customers in that period (the sale which generated some of that cash may have occurred in a different reporting period). When cash comes in from sales or from people paying you back, that cash comes in "from operations". That is all of the cash the business received from its business operations in that period. The cash you spend in paying bills during the period for operations (overhead, payroll, interest, COGS related bills) in the period represents cash out from operations. The net of these activities represents the net cash flow (+/-) from operations.

*Investment Cash Flow (ICF)* - This represents items such as the purchase or sale of property, plant or equipment items which are assets which may be subject to depreciation or the purchase or sale of long term certificates of deposit or other long term investment vehicles. The purchase or sale of intangible items such as "good will", patents or contract rights may also be listed in this section. If you sell old equipment, that would be a source of investment cash in-flow. Cash expended to buy inventory is investment cash out-flow. For example, you buy fifty cases of pens to sell them, you're using cash to get that inventory on board - that's investing. If your investment goes up – cash goes down. If your investment goes down, (by collecting cash for selling assets), cash goes up.

*Financing Cash Flow (FCF)* - The last section of the cash flow statement is cash acquired from borrowing money or paying back the <u>principal</u> of loans (not the interest – which is an expense in the OCF section). Borrowing more improves cash. Paying back the principle portion of loans takes away from cash. The contribution of additional capital by the owners would also be recorded in the financing section of the cash flow statement as cash in.

*Starting and Ending Balance* - At the beginning of the period, this is the amount of cash and cash equivalents*, available to the business at the start of the reporting period. (*Cash equivalents are generally low risk securities that can be quickly liquidated if needed). The cash flow statement will show adds and deletes to that starting balance during the reporting period from 3 categories of sources (Operating, Investing and Financing) and conclude with an ending balance of cash.

At a minimum, you need to understand the balance sheet, the P&L, and the cash flow statements in your business.

# FUTURE PROJECTIONS

The previous reports are necessary for your business, however they all tell us what's happened in the past. If running a business was like driving a bus, most business owners are driving by only looking into the rear view mirrors. To make faster progress and to get safely to your destination of success, you need a windshield to see where you're going and key gauges on your dashboard to know how you're progressing in real time so you can make the necessary adjustments while you're driving.

Your budget or financial plan is your windshield and your navigation system ("Prepare to turn right in 1.5 miles"). If your dashboard blacked out while driving, how would you react? Think about the information you'd be missing. How would you know how much gas (think cash) is left in the tank? Have you ever been too busy to stop to  get gas? Some businesses do that. They keep on trucking till they "can't go no more". At that point, they're sitting along the side of the road somewhere calling for help with a lot of upset paying passengers (who will probably never book travel on your bus line again). Your fuel is your cash. What "dashboard" indicators are in your business to monitor the status of cash flow? You might also need to know how fast you're traveling and the engine speed (so you can shift gears as needed) and you might want some indicators if you get low on oil before the engine seizes.

# OMG! What's The Focus?

A budget and a set of KPIs (Key Performance Indicators – your "dashboard") helps keep you on track. If you knew you needed 50 sales at a certain dollar level per week to achieve your goal, then you could effectively monitor sales throughout the week and make adjustments at the end of the week to stay *focused* on your goals. You would know exactly whether you were on course or not. The alternative is to *focus* exclusively on your financial reports. But that only gives you information from last month, instead of updating important information in the here and now aligned with your planned results.

In a complex organization, each different department's KPI (Key Performance or Predictive Indicator) is what links up to the overall goal. Let's say your goal is 30 sales per week. Let's assume you know, from measuring, that on average, every other face-to-face with a qualified prospect produces a sale. If your sales team does not go out and prospect with at least 60 people, you're not going to have 30 sales that week. So you can measure whether the sales department is reaching the appointment goal of meeting 60 people. If they don't meet the goal, you're not going to hit your 30. Now by mid-week, at the latest, you can take some action to help get the team back on track and they know clearly where to *focus* their attention. Turns out two sales guys were on vacation the same week. It took them a week to get back in the swing of things, so for two weeks the team did not hit the face to face goal and sales suffered. Where was everybody else to help pick up the load? Where was the manager jumping in? If you had a proper KPI report, you (or your manager) could have intervened in the first week when the volume of appointments dropped. Otherwise, how are you supposed to be warned without a blinking red indicator on your dashboard? Teams will *focus* on what the owner *focuses* on (and asks about).

**FREE RESOURCE
DOWNLOAD**
Projection Tool
www.actioncoachtampabay.com/pro

# CASH GAP

Understanding Cash Gap is another way to predict the future performance of your business. Many businesses purchase their inventory in bulk. That's cash out the door. The inventory arrives, available to sell. Depending on the business, it might take some time to sell that inventory. Now let's say your customers can pay you in 30 days, because maybe that's common in your industry. Those 30 days are called a "sales term". The time it took between paying for the inventory and then awaiting receipt of the inventory, selling it and finally collecting the cash for the sale—that holding time—is called the "cash gap". The gap between the out flow of cash for inventory purchase and the cash in from collecting on the sale of that inventory.

If you want to grow your business, that cash gap needs to be funded somehow. Otherwise, growing the business could actually put you out of business, because you could run out of cash. Cash Gap is a common problem in many businesses so monitoring and projecting cash flow should be a critical *focus* in every businesses. The first step in solving a complex problem is measuring and tracking the key steps in the process. Second is looking for the best predictive indicators of outcome (that can be measured "real time") followed by planning for improvement and disciplined execution. Then "rinse and repeat" – Plan – Do – Study – Act.

## 5 WAYS TO PROFITABILITY

There are 5 key areas that drive profitability and *focus* in any business. There are *three things* every single business wants: *more customers, more revenues,* and *more profit.* All three of these things are a product of something else. You can't just go out and get more customers, or revenues, or profits. They are the results of other activities that you can measure and improve.

**The Five Proven Ways to Increase Your Business Profits**

Number of Leads
x
Conversion Rate
=
Customers
x
# of Transactions
x
Average Dollar Sale
=
Revenue
x
Profit Margins
=
*$Profit$*

***Leads*** - If you want more customers, for example, you need to first get leads. To get more leads, you need to first measure your current performance (get a dashboard of Key Predictive Indicators -KPIs). As a result of your analysis of your business and the needs of your customers, develop a marketing plan (much more on that in the next chapter) to communicate your value proposition that matters to *them*.

Once you consistently execute and measure your plan's results you will begin generating more interest – **leads** for your business.

### *Leads* x *Conversions* = **Customers**

*Conversion Rate* – But to get money from and the opportunity to meet the needs of your leads, they must be converted into paying customers. The business process for conversion is sales. **Ideal sales people and sales systems *focus* on professionally assisting people to make great buying decisions** (more on that in the sales chapter of this book). Measuring conversion rates followed by documenting and training incessantly on the best methods for assisting leads to make great decisions are the keys to improvement.

### **Customers x *# Transactions* x *Avg. $ Sale* = Revenue**

*Number of Transactions* – This is the number of times your customers do business with you on average in a particular reporting period. One of the greatest opportunities in most businesses lies not in working hard to get brand new people, unfamiliar with your brand and uniqueness to buy a first time but to get previous customers to buy more frequently from you. That's what the "# of Transactions 5-Way Strategy" is all about. There are numerous strategies available to every business to improve # of Transactions.

*Average Dollar Sale* – This is the average amount a customer spends during a single transaction. Again, once you've gotten someone to agree to buy, you have a huge opportunity not only to get them to come back more frequently but also to increase the amount they spend when they buy. How much, on average, are your customers spending now? How good is your team at selling all of your products by informing customers of all you do and giving them opportunities to buy more of what they want and need? McDonalds is a master of this game. You've heard it. "Do you want fries with that? How about an apple pie? What else can I get for you?" These lines are from a script to get customers thinking, "What else do I want while I'm already here?" They also make it easy to buy "packages" – You: "I'll have a number 3". Attendant: "Great, would you like to get the larger drink for just 50 cents more?".

In working with one of our online media companies, once we re-structured their "packages" to make it easier for customers to buy their revenue and profit took off. They are growing 125% month over month and are adding on new employees and increasing their office space. This is when the business gets really fun!

### Revenue x *Margin* = Profit

*Margin* – In this final 5-Way strategy, we're focused on improving our margin percent because your revenue (income) generated by the other 4 strategies multiplied by your average Gross Profit% (or Margin%) equals your Gross Profit. Earlier in the chapter, in our review of P&L, we discussed Gross Profit - aka Gross Margin or just "Margin" (Gross Profit = Gross Revenue – COGS). We also explained why margins are so critical to growth. Here's what we said: *Once your Gross Profit is sufficient to pay your Fixed Expenses, every penny in excess Gross Profit creates your Net Operating Profit. Since Fixed Expenses are relatively "Fixed", as long as you manage your overhead expenses, all growth in Gross Profit results in more Profit!* One of the easiest and most direct ways to improve margin is to raise prices and to stop discounting. Strategies to reduce COGS and/or changing product mix (with more emphasis on higher margin, less competitive lines) can also be very effective.

The 5-Ways takes advantage of the compounding effect. Compounding refers to generating additional gains on top of or from previous gains. So, for example, if we improve leads and improve conversion rate, the gains in customers from the conversion rate gains are not just from the original number of leads but also the new leads gained from that improvement. If we now improve # Transactions & Avg. $ Sale those gains will be "compounded" by the gains in Customers from the Leads and Conversion rate strategies. And finally, any improvement to Margins will be "compounded" by the increases generated by the compounded gains in the other 4 (Leads, Conv. Rate, #Transactions & Avg. $ sale).

## With just a 10% Increase

| | | | |
|---|---|---|---|
| Number of Leads | 4,000 | 4,400 | 10% |
| x | x | x | x |
| Conversion Rate | 25% | 27.5% | 10% |
| = | = | = | = |
| Customers | 1,000 | 1,210 | 21% |
| x | x | x | x |
| # of Transactions | 2 | 2.5 | 10% |
| x | x | x | x |
| Average Dollar Sale | $100 | $110 | 10% |
| = | = | = | = |
| Revenue | $200,000 | $292,820 | 46% |
| x | x | x | x |
| Profit Margins | 25% | 25% | 10% |
| = | = | = | = |
| $Profit$ | $50,000 | $80,525.50 | 61% |

As an example of how this can work in any business, look at the illustration of a small business that made just a very modest improvement of 10% in each of the 5-Ways strategies. The results are a 21% improvement to number of customers, a 46% improvement to revenue and a 61% improvement in Profit. It's easy to see why Benjamin Franklin said that: "Compound interest is the greatest mathematical discovery of mankind."

Most businesses never hit 61% improvement in profit because their efforts are entirely directed at *one or two* of these 5 key areas for improvement. Most commonly, business owners focus on growing leads, the most expensive and time consuming of the five. If you focused on improving each area by a little, you could greatly increase your profitability.

> **FREE RESOURCE DOWNLOAD**
>
> 5 Ways Tool
> www.actioncoachtampabay.com/five

What's the most efficient 5-Way strategy to start with? As we said, many leaders tend to start with leads. They think they just need more volume, when in fact more volume means more hours, more employees, more effort. A smart business owner thinks about making more money with less hours and with less quantity.

# 1$^{st}$ GROSS MARGIN

The first of the five to start with is the last one: gross margin. Every customer that flows through your business process will generate a gross margin. And improving margins usually has no cost other than the time and effort associated with understanding and tracking the financial drivers of the business. Look first at pricing, frivolous discounting, product margin mix and COGS.

# 2$^{nd}$ CONVERSION RATE

The second area is conversion rate. You have to first evaluate who's following up or "taking" the leads your current marketing efforts are producing. Many business owners produce leads just to have the phone answered by grumpy grandmothers or young employees with bad attitudes. This is a big opportunity for improvement. All the time and money spent to get that phone call and the person answering completely turned off the prospect. Who among us has not had that experience in calling other businesses? So why not improve your sales conversion system before you crank out more leads? You won't have to spend as much money on lead generation when you're converting a higher number of your existing leads to customers. There might even be a pot of gold in leads that said no the first time or never responded to a proposal or bid.

## 3rd & 4th REVENUE FROM CUSTOMERS

The third and fourth areas both relate to the revenue from existing customers. This is more than a pot of gold – it's potentially a whole goldmine business owners are missing. We can't tell you how many business could but don't keep track and/or don't regularly communicate with previous customers. In today's age we have Social Media: Facebook, LinkedIn, Twitter, YouTube and all sorts of customer loyalty systems. These are all major customer relationship tools. How well are you managing these as databases? And getting them to come back is just part of the opportunity. They already know, like and trust you or they would have never bought from you in the first place so what else might you offer that would be of value? Have you ever had a customer say something like: "I didn't know you did that or had that product". How could you make it easier to buy? – Packages, referral strategies, special events, etc.

## 5th LEADS

Finally, the last of the five ways should be leads. Truly understanding how to market from a targeted, measured perspective. We'll talk about that very soon in the *Marketing* chapter.

## MARGIN MASTERY

Maybe you own an office supply business. Not only are you selling pencils, you're selling paper, pens, staplers, computers, printers, office equipment, etc. Each of those have a different cost of goods sold with a different margin potential. Maybe pencils have a 30% margin, yet the computers have an 80% margin (probably the other way around). Either way, understanding the different margin levels is critical information.

We've seen many business that sold products, unknowingly, at a loss. This happens when the negative margin of that product or service is "hidden" by positive margins in some other line of products or services. If the business were to increase the volume of that negative margin category, they could grow themselves into bankruptcy. Unfortunately we've seen this happen more than once. The challenge is understanding the margin generated in each sale or at the very least, in each category of products. A business might have multiple verticals. A printing company might sell large format printing. They may also sell specialty items. Each of those products have drastically different margins. When they understand margins, they can strategize and plan for deployment of resources to the part of the business they want to grow, and which needs work to improve its margin. The business, overall, is improved with this type of intelligence, insight and *focus*.

It's also critical to understand the impact of discounting. Discounting is a very common but usually damaging practice. For example, if you sell a product for $100 and it costs you $60 to produce, you're gross margin is $40, or 40%. Since many sales teams have permission to discount up to 10% to close a sale, let's look at the true impact of a 10% discount in this case. Since the cost of goods doesn't change, If you give a 10% discount on a product priced at $100 with a 40% margin, that discount of $10 only applies to your "mark-up" of $40. The result is a reduction in your gross profit of 25%. From $40 to $30 is a 25% discount to your profit. Your sales team assumes you can make it up in volume – if you give a discount, their theory goes, more people will buy – making up the difference. The math does not support that theory – You would have to increase your volume by 35% just to get back to where you were before the discount. If you only started out with a 20% margin ($100 product with $80 in COGS), a 10% discount would result in giving away 50% of your profit on that product. You would have to have a 100% increase in volume to get back to the margins you were generating before you gave the 10% discount.

On the other hand, if you increased the price of your product by just 10%, most consumers will not notice or mind, but you sure will. In your product with the 40% margin, you've now improved your profit by 14%. ($110 dollar price with a $60 COGS). And if you only have a 20% margin and you increase it by 10%, that's a 36% increase in your profit. Big difference.

Lastly, understanding your "Break-Even" and "Target Break Even" is essential for knowing what it will take in measurable activity each week and each day to achieve your goals. Now our "bus" would have a beautiful windshield and a truly sophisticated and effective dashboard to create the *focus* that is needed. Monthly Break-even is the amount of gross revenue (total Income) you need to generate per month to generate a zero net profit. In other words, what is the revenue required to cover all expenses – COGS and fixed expenses. Your estimated monthly break even can be calculated by dividing your average monthly fixed expenses by your Avg. gross margin %. (BE = Fixed Expense/Gross margin %). Monthly break even estimates the Gross revenue required each month to earn a zero net profit.

But no business wants zero net profit. So let's calculate a "Target Break-even". Take your average monthly fixed expenses as before but now, let's further determine the profit you want to have in each month. Let's say you want a profit level of $10,000 per month in your business. Add $10,000 to your previous average fixed expenses and divide by your average gross Margin% as before. Your "Target Break-even" indicates the Gross revenue required each month to earn a $10,000 Net profit. If you divide your new Target Break-even calculation by 4, you now know your estimated target for revenue each week and can easily calculate Avg. revenue required per day.

**The Backwards Five Ways:** Divide your monthly calculated target for Gross revenue (to produce your desired profit) by your current Avg $ sale and you can now know how many transactions you need, and then customers. Using an estimate or actual measure of Conversion Rate, you can even calculate how many leads (qualified inquires or face-to-face meetings completed) would be required each week to achieve your target. Now take the 5-ways Formula and start plugging in your numbers starting at the bottom with your targeted gross profit and revenue.

Think about what you've learned in this chapter. Where will you now choose to place your *focus*? – if you can make small improvements to any or several of the 5-Ways elements, you could achieve your goals with far fewer leads and new customers – that's working smarter and using the leverage of compounding to your advantage. Pretty soon, you're thinking in the future and above the line. What could I do and how could I do it and by when? You're developing highly effective KPIs that can tell your team what to look at every day and how to design a marketing and sales plan to achieve those plans. Now you're in more control. You can determine every day how much volume is needed to generate the profits you have envisioned and chosen to achieve.

## CHAPTER 4
### KEY THOUGHTS

◎ Cash vs. Accrual Accounting
◎ The Big 3: Balance Sheet, Profit & Loss
   Statement, Cash Flow Report
◎ Future Budget Projections
◎ 5 Ways to Increase Profit
◎ Cash Gap

### OMG! WHAT'S THE FOCUS?
### ACTION STEPS

1) _____
2) _____
3) _____
4) _____
5) _____

### CONTINUED THINKING

◎ Instant Cashflow - Sugars
◎ Instant Profit - Sugars
◎ The Ultimate Blueprint for an Insanely
   Successful Business - Cunningham

# 5

# *Marketing*

*"Remarkable means it's worth making a remark about."* – **Seth Godin**

The three critically important components of marketing are niche, target segment(s) and measure & test. In this chapter, you will uncover how to create a strong niche and unique selling proposition so you can stop competing on price and start competing on value. You will learn the 5 questions to answer in order to create a targeted campaign that will make you forget about market share and start capitalizing on wallet share. And finally, you will learn the importance of setting up measurement for your marketing, what to measure, and how to start testing to arrive at having an unlimited marketing budget.

## DEFINING MARKETING

When the question of "what is marketing?" is raised to hundreds of business owners – the most common responses are advertising, how you communicate your product or services, and awareness to get someone to buy from you. The fact is marketing is all of these things and more – and that fact often makes marketing seem overwhelming, complicated, expensive and challenging. Jay Conrad Levinson, known as the Father of Guerrilla Marketing is seen as one of the greatest marketing authorities of all time with 58 books in 62 nations and 21 million copies  sold and is the strategist behind brand memes you know like Marlboro Man, the Jolly Green Giant, Tony The Tiger, Pillsbury Dough Boy, Allstate's You're In Good Hands, and many more. Levinson defines marketing as "absolutely every bit of contact any part of your business  has with any segment of the public". This broad reaching definition helps you realize it is the first impression, the car you drive, how your employees answer "what do you do?", what your office looks like when someone pulls up, what impression your website or logo gives... all of these are small details that market your business to the public.

*"I've written 58 books on Guerrilla Marketing and sold 21 million copies in 62 nations. When I write books and tell people what to do about marketing, **I know that 90% of those people will read it, love the ideas, and not do anything about it.** They just don't have the ability to take action. Guerrilla Marketing is not a spectator sport, it is all about action. I revere companies like **ActionCOACH** because **without these people***

*much of what I write about and speak about would be for not* because *people won't do anything about it."*

*– Jay Conrad Levinson, Father of Guerilla Marketing*

## SWOT ANALYSIS

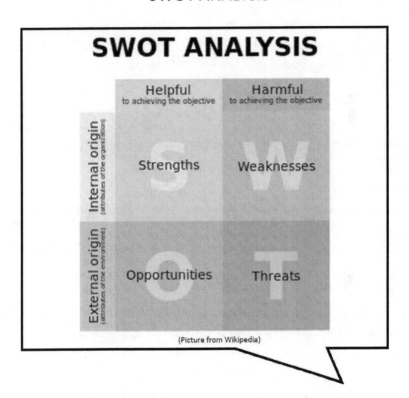

(Picture from Wikipedia)

Even the most inexperienced marketers have often heard of a SWOT analysis and for those of you who have not, you are about to learn a wonderful tool for stepping back and reviewing your business from a tree-top perspective. S.W.O.T. is an acronym standing for:

**S**trengths
**W**eaknesses
**O**pportunities
**T**reats

Strengths and weaknesses primarily have to do with internal aspects in the business. For example, some strengths might be that you deliver very quickly on promises or your packaging is effective and appealing for products. Your weaknesses might be that you don't make enough time for training, or you don't have a lot of systems written down so follow up is slow and often chaotic.

The other two portions of the SWOT Analysis relate to opportunities and threats going on externally and would be happening whether or not your business was in existence or not. For example, a threat might be a lot of industry competition that is saturating your demographic area. Another threat might be a recent law change that effects industry regulations on how businesses like yours can market. An example opportunity would be that other competitors have low online ratings or recent studies show your area wants more options when buying in your sector.

Getting a high level perspective on your marketplace and your specific business allows you to identify competitive advantages by matching external opportunities with internal strengths. It also allows you to see the areas that you need to consider converting from a treat or weakness into an opportunity or strength or at least strategically lessen the impact of them over the long-run. It's a great activity to do first and foremost before you get in to the nitty-gritty details of marketing – and a tool well worth reviewing as situational analysis changes overtime.

## DELIVERY INCONSISTENCIES AND YOUR USP

You may be wondering what delivery inconsistency has to do with marketing and why it is even in this section – looking at the USP's (Unique Selling Point) for FedEx and Domino's Pizza the answer becomes clear.

First let's start with a simple definition of USP, short for unique selling proposition or unique selling point. The term was first coined by Rosser Reeves in his book published in 1961, *Reality in Advertising.* Reeves defines a USP as having three parts:

1. Must say "Buy this product, for this specific benefit."

2. Must be one the competition cannot or does not offer – it must be truly unique.

3. Must be strong enough to move the masses.

There are of course two parts to creating your USP – the promise and the process or the delivery. You must have something unique that you can promise your customers will get when they buy your product and services – and then you need to actually be able to deliver on that promise which is where *delivery* comes into play.

Do you recall the well-known USP example of FedEx? The tune that so elegantly filled a dependable overnight delivery need in the marketplace - "when your package absolutely, positively has to get there overnight". If FedEx simply promised to get it there overnight but was never able to deliver on that promise how would it be any different or unique than all the other postal service options?

Now think about your industry and what inconsistencies, risks, or frustrations your customers are already expecting when dealing with your *type* of business? For example, when you go to a dentist, most would say they expect long wait times, pain, unpleasant smells, sound of drills, and a large bill waiting for them at the end. Take a moment to list the top five frustrations your customers have with your business or with your industry.

If you don't have delivery consistency in your business in the top five areas you just listed, should you start spending money and time on marketing? Here's one way of thinking about it – can you take a bath if you leave the plug out of the tub? Until you correct the inconsistencies in your delivery, it will be much like turning on the marketing faucet and forgetting to put the plug in the tub to capture and retain those pricey leads and customers. Ramping up more volume will simply result in more complaints, more customer service payroll expense, and less referrals. You don't even have to be the best quality – just look at McDonald's. They don't have the best hamburger in the world, but no matter where you are in the world you'll get it made the same way by teenagers who can't even make their beds in the morning.

Here's the bonus to you for identifying the key areas of frustrations and plugging up your tub by getting consistency in your delivery: you become the preferred choice. Imagine if you became the dentist that offered headphones to eliminate the sound, odorless products, affordable packages with payment plans, and a no-wait guarantee or your exam is free. If this was your dental business, all you did was work to provide the very things that frustrate your customers when they do business with you and your competitors.

Here are some of the benefit of doing this:

- You are making it crystal clear why they should choose you over another provider.

- Your clients may even pay a little more for your

product or service.

- You would begin to tell the story to your friends and business associates so they refer to you more.

- You would have super *focused* on your USP when communicating with your marketing materials.

A quick reminder of Reeve's USP point number two: Must be one the competition cannot or does not offer – it must be *truly* unique. To be sure you are on the right track, you will want to conduct some investigative work on your competition. We call this market research. Learn more about who they are, what they offer, what their pricing looks like, what are they doing to differentiate themselves, what targets or audiences do they work with and what kind of warranties or guarantees do they offer.

Another source for market research is your own team of employees, customers, suppliers, and community that have known you or have done business with you. Ask a variety of people with different perspectives on your business to write a short benefits list. Simply answering the question, "What are all the benefits of doing business with us?" Don't compare notes until you are  done because it will be interesting to see how many things you have in common from your research and how many varying ideas that will surface.

At the beginning of this section, I mentioned the USP of Domino's Pizza which you may or may not remember contained a guarantee; "you get fresh, hot pizza delivered to your door in 30 minutes or less – or it's free." In a completely saturated market of pizza shops on every corner, they were able to fill the need for busy, working mothers with hungry kids after school and with a strong guarantee illuminated the risk, frustration, and usual inconsistency of turnaround time that existed in the pizza industry at that time. Just like the dentist example of no wait or your exam is free, what could you guarantee in your business to create confidence in your ability to delivery consistently on something your customer needs and wants?

The number one myth that keeps businesses from creating a guarantee is the fear that you will be taken advantage of when the fact is the positive impacts far exceed any scamming. Besides creating confidence around your consistent delivery, the best thing about a guarantee is you get to choose the terms and words.  This  means you can use your guarantee as a positioning statement on how to get the best results from you and set up clear expectations of the outcome they will experience by working with you.

## MARKETING CAMPAIGNS: PICKING ONE TARGET

Now that you've done some high level thinking and some research on your competition, it's time to embark on a targeted, highly *focused* marketing campaign. Marketing campaigns are all about speaking directly to each slice or chuck of the pie (prospects and future customers) rather than spreading your limited resources and bland message across the entire pie. It's not about market share – capturing as many leads as possible. A *focused* marketing campaign for one target is all about wallet share – getting lower quantity, high quality and  profitable customers who come back often and bring their friends. This doesn't mean you must turn away customers. It only means that you are going to *focus* your money, time and energy on speaking directly to a target audience so your message is seen, understood, and acted upon by more people who are a perfect fit for what you offer. The next logical question becomes who is your target audience or audiences? There are, however, *four* additional questions that need to be answered before your targeted and *focused* marketing campaign is complete.

# THE 5 QUESTIONS

When someone says *marketing*, the first place most of us love to talk about are all the actions we are taking, the networking we are attending, the advertising we are placing, the online marketing strategizing, the social media we are using, the direct mail piece we are sending or the speaking engagements we are presenting – you get the picture. The fact is that all of those actions are answering question number *five* before question *one*, *two*, *three*, or *four* have even been discussed. The order of these *five* questions are important because without first *focusing* on the who are you targeting, how can you know where to find them? The where comes later as well as the what they want to buy or why they should buy from you? It's amazing when you start from the beginning of the story – sometimes the ending changes a little or changes completely. Let's start off at the beginning before we jump to the fifth question of how do we communicate with our target...

# Question #1: WHO?

What if you thought of your current clients or desired ideal future clients in terms of A, B, C, and D?

**A = Awesome**
**B = Basic**
**C = Can't Deal With**
**D = Wish I Could Hit Delete Button.**

"D" stands for delete – the clients described by their lack of payment, their incessant questions, their lack of follow up and follow through, their continual complaints, their need after need that is not a part of what you originally agreed to and of course, they are the ones who give you the two and half stars review on google after you went above and beyond to please them. Does this sound familiar?

Although the reverse is true of an "A" client – they are awesome because they are thought of as a friend, they are fun to be around, they are so grateful to buy from you, they rave about you every chance they get, they quickly forgive your mistakes, they come back to buy again without any prompting, they buy the most expensive products, they pay in advance, anything you suggest they buy, they stay in contact and invite you to their events and they give you the most tear-jerking sincere google reviews. Do you want more of these clients? *Focusing* on this type of client would give you more time and lower the consumption of your resources.

Now that we are clear on the drastic differences between an "A" client and a "D" client – using the 80/20 rule, here is the big *ah-ha* moment for you. The theme of a "D" client is that they take up 80 percent of your time because of the extra effort it takes to get paid and keep them somewhat but never completely happy. Versus the A's and B's who are happy with what you give them and never ask for more than what they think is *fair* take up about 20 percent of your time.

Although we've missed one big component, what other value do the "A" clients bring you? Yes, their other A and B friends. Those referrals that bring great wallet share to your business in easy delivery, delighted customers, successful outcomes and bigger, long-term profit returns. So, why is it that you are choosing to spend 80 percent of your time with D's when you could be nurturing, thanking, and collecting referrals from your A's and B's? Now that you've had that *ah-ha* your business could be changed forever. Ask yourself, how can you start referring away your "D" clients and what competitor would gratefully take them with open arms?

Now that the D's are gone. Let's *focus* your attention back on clearly defining who are your "A" client target(s). There are several lenses or angles to view this to come up with some great target segments. One is to get a list of your top 20% of clients who are currently giving you 80% of your sales. That list can be very telling as far as what targets best fit for your business so you can grow the number that will work with you. *Second* is to do some digging into your margins to find out what products or services deliver you the highest returns. This is getting a list of customers who buy the highest volume of your highest margin offering and therefore are the 20% giving you 80% of your profit rather than just revenue. The power of knowing your highest margin product or services also allows you to think outside the box of other targets you might not be currently servicing but would be a great fit and have a need for that high margin offering. *Thirdly*, you can use all the work you've done to research your competitive advantage and USP to reverse engineer who would really get excited that you offer that unique solution to that inconsistency in the market place. Think about Domino's Pizza, they targeted busy, single-parent mothers because they were a perfect fit for their 30 minute delivery guarantee. *Lastly*, if you cover a specific demographical area, you can do some research on who is in your area. It might surprise you when you actually look at the facts and help you pinpoint targets that would be a great fit for your offering you didn't think of through any of the other three perspective angles.

Once you have a target or several target audiences in mind – it's time to pick one to *focus* on at a time. It's the *focus* on one target and one only per campaign that is the most challenging to do yet will bring you the highest wallet share return. You will need to drill down into the specifics of that one target you have chosen to *focus* on. You will need to get a list of them filtered by specific descriptors like age, gender, location, buying behaviors, educational level, job type, job title, household earnings, family status, credit score, hobbies, key words or phrases, level of knowledge of your offering, and many more. You also need to begin filtering on all of the aspects that make an "A" client awesome including preferences, affordability, time restrictions, attitude, desire or need, connections, communication style and values.

Let's take an example target audience as we continue on answering the *five* questions to build a marketing campaign. Let's say you have a plumbing business and you've figured out your highest paying client is someone who installs a new water heater and would understand the value of having a maintenance plan. You narrow down the list of targets to homes of a specific age, home value, neighborhoods, families with 1 or more children (more people the bigger the system), 2 or more bathroom homes, and women more specifically stay at home mothers in the age range of 29-45.

## Question #2: WHERE?

The second crucial question to answer is where? Not where are they located – where are they found in the highest concentration? Where would you find a lot of mothers that are busy and have a lot of people in the household in these income areas? Who are the other people targeting them? Who else would be helping them to maintain the value and functionality of their home? What else would they buy on a regular basis? Where would they go for fun? What do they like to read or watch or listen to? What do their kids like to do or where would they regularly go? What schools do their kids go to? This list would include Rupert the local electrician, a homeowners association, soccer teams, after school tutors, or a local grocery store. You might ask a more specific question like where would they be in the highest concentration when their water heater breaks? Think water restoration companies, mold clean up, or the internet under key phrases like "replacement water heater", "what to do if your water heater leaks", etc. Once you answer where are they in the highest concentration, a new light is shined on more effective, smart ways and methods of reaching them in a more *focused* and targeted fashion.

## Question #3: WHAT?

The third question to ask yourself is what do they want to buy from you and what could you offer them to get them to buy from you? Answering this question starts with listing all the products and services they would want to buy from you and some of the benefits associated with buying them. The second part of this question is always the challenge – to write a compelling offer that elicits action. From time to time a business owner will remember an offer they used to run in the past like a $5.00 off coupon that brought in 50 new customers but they haven't run it in years. Sometimes business owners have only used weak offers similar to their competition like free estimates or free consultations. If either of these are *you*, there is some work to be done. You need to create a list of offers that are valuable to your target and something they would have spent money on – a free estimate or consultation in most cases is expected to be free so it doesn't hold any monetary value. It doesn't always need to be a discount either – it can be a gift, content, trial, easy return, exclusivity, something scarce or in limited supply, seasonal, limited production, *As Seen On TV*, best seller, or most popular. Remember it doesn't always have to do with your business – it just needs to be of value to your target so they will take action on it.

A young, stay-at-home mother with younger children might be looking to buy a plumbing maintenance program so they don't have to think about scheduling your next plumbing visit. You just put them right into a program and come on a regular basis to avoid another water heater break down. It might also include a service where, if a kid did flush something down a toilet, there were so many allowances each year to come out and do a flush. There might also be a program where you had multiple different options for the water heater, depending on how many people use it and care about water efficiency, and you were prepared with those different options. That target might also be interested in having a water filtration system installed to protect her children from harmful contaminants in the water.

Your list of offers might include a free water heater test to see when it will need replaced causing them to take a first step or give you a trial. You might also offer to do a free water quality test to show what the standard is now and what a filtration system would do. You might offer to give the mother a certificate for a free manicure and pedicure at a high-end nail salon in the area while you are installing her new water heater. You could offer dinner for four delivered to her door on the day of the new system installation.

Think outside the box as it doesn't necessarily have to be really expensive, it just has to be something that gets their attention and is specific to that particular target. You are already spending all your time and money taking actions to market to them and gain their attention – why not maximize the return by finding offers that create a desire and urgency to take action? Part of making a profitable offer also has to do with understanding your measurement, which we're going to talk about later in this chapter.

# Question #4: WHY?

The fourth question of why relates back to your unique selling proposition, your guarantee, and answers the question why should they do business with you rather than your competitor? Using our plumbing business and the busy mother target with a burst water heater, think about what is the top benefit you offer, or inconsistencies that she wants to avoid when choosing a plumber? You could offer a 100% satisfaction guarantee that you will fix, replace, or repair until she is 100% satisfied. You could guarantee fast turn-around time of the install by saying "same day install" or "I will show up on time or it's on me". You could be the clean plumber that brings in a cleaning crew to clean the house after the job is complete. You could be the well-dressed plumber that comes in a tux and bearing gifts or flowers.

Think about the needs, wants, frustrations or inconsistencies for your target when buying from your industry and start being the one with the solution, the guarantee, and the unique offering that will attract them. Remember, the second most important part of finding a powerful promise is to make sure you can consistently deliver on that with a great process.

**FREE RESOURCE DOWNLOAD**
USP and Guarantee Exercise
www.actioncoachtampabay.com/niche

# Question #5: HOW?

The fifth question is always the favorite: how to best communicate with our target? Now that you've answered the earlier questions, you understand who your target is, where to find them in the highest concentration, what you are offering them and what they want to buy from you, as well as why you are unique to them. This makes answering the question of how to communicate with them much easier and highly focused.

Taking the example of the mother looking for a plumber – the way you would normally communicate with your customer might not best fit how to communicate with a busy mother. First think of all the ways she takes in information on a regular basis or all the ways she learns about plumbers to use. She is regularly using a smart phone that includes Facebook, internet searches, text, calls, friends (referrals), and numbers of other providers like electrician or air conditioning or cleaning lady for example. She takes regular trips to her grocery store, children's school and after school activities as well as reading her kid's school newsletter – maybe even participating in the PTA. Start figuring out all the different media types that would be best to communicate with your target including phone, email, TV, radio, print, online, social media, mail, word of mouth, convention, networking, referrals, etc. Then start brainstorming specific strategies or places to get in front of a high concentration of your target like the media type Facebook and then strategies like Facebook ads, Facebook groups, Facebook business pages also targeting mothers in the target area, Facebook contest with a prize mother's want, etc. You are now ready to learn how to store all of these ideas in an organized 10 x 10 strategy "playbook".

# 10 X 10 STRATEGY

Have you ever found out about a great charity event that attracts hundreds of your target audience but you need a place to remember the name of it for later in the year? Are you one of those thinkers who is always coming up with creative strategies to reach your target but don't have time immediately to take action? This is just one of the benefits of creating a 10 x 10 strategy "playbook". It's meant to be a place for you to brainstorm, place ideas, look at it throughout the game, and play it all throughout the season to reach your target audience. If you're watching a football game and you see the coach standing on the sidelines, he's got this laminated sheet of paper, but what is on that laminated sheet? It's the plays that have been designed for that specific team, that specific *focus* in the game. It's not their entire playbook, it's the plays that they think are going to be most effective. Do you think the coach uses every one of those plays on that play sheet? No, he has an idea of the first couple he's going to run at the beginning of the game, under certain circumstances, then he watches to see what works.

If the coach calls a "slant right" off the right tackle, and that play starts going for decent yardage, how often is he going to keep up that play? Until they find a way to stop it – over and over and over again. So your 10 x 10 is like that playbook - it's something you've designed, it's a set of plays you thought about in advance that might work to effectively get to your target. And then you're going to decide which plays you'll run first and then you'll measure them. Which one do you think will be the most effective out of that group of plays? If you go back at the end of a quarter and certain things aren't working, you can make adjustments; you have other "plays" you can try to see if they will work better.

# Example 10 x 10
## 10% x 10 Ways = 100%

| | Networking | Seminars | Referrals | Speaking | Email Contact | PR & Materials | Lead FU | Website | Alliances | Direct Mail |
|---|---|---|---|---|---|---|---|---|---|---|
| 1 | STP Chbr | Buy/Sell Build | 6 Steps | No STP Chbr Orientation | Intro to New Leads | Networking | Ad Critiques | Online Registration | CFO | Sales Genie |
| 2 | PH Chbr | Big Name Speaker | BizRICH | NPI Regional Amex | Event Calendar Link | BABM Keys Article | Diag/Biz Assessment | Optimized Conversion Page | CPA | FL Barter Mbrship |
| 3 | UTB Chbr | Sales | Growth CLUB | BB&T | Other Upcoming Events | Announcements | Bold Calls | Speaking Topics/ Service | Biz Attorney | Chbr Directories |
| 4 | ACG | 6 Steps | Profit CLUB | Rotary | Offers/ Incentives | Upcoming Events | Footcanvasing | Articles | Banks | Alliance Database |
| 5 | SPYP | Networking | Surveys | BNI | Ways to Refer | Spring Planning | Feedback thu Call | Recommended Reading List | Financial Planners | CPA Clients |
| 6 | NPI | SPYP | CPA Gifts | PH Chbr | Articles | Economic Stim/Timely | GrowthCLUB | BizRich Resource Pg | Business Brokers | Brokers |
| 7 | BNI | Timely Topic | Give More | UTB Chbr | Client Recognition | PR Media Pack | Referrals | Picture Gallery | Marketing | Velocity IQ Mailer |
| 8 | REIC | Host Ben | Reward Program (CNE) | ACG | Community Event Calendar | Intro to ACP for Corps | Strategic/ Marketing Plan Review | Video Testimonials | Web Design | Hoovers 3-5Mil |
| 9 | TTF | 5 Ways | Alliances | Centre Club | Target Messages | Strategic Alliance Pkg | 5 Steps Tickets | Simple Service Offering | Newspaper/ Mag | Industry Specific |
| 10 | PEA | Time Mgmt | Enroll Others | Human Resource Dir | Alliance Spotlight | Resolutions | Team Workshops | Specific Domain Names | Insurance Agent | Geographic |

It's a great tool to pull back out when you are resetting your 90 days goals to review what plays from the sheet worked and what plays you want to play or test in the coming quarter. To create your 10 x 10 playbook on a sheet of paper, all you need is a table with 10 columns and 11 rows. Along the top row, each column is labeled with your media types that are best for communicating with your specific target audience - like the mother seeking a new water heater from a plumber. These media types might include networking,  email, phone, mail, print, online, social media, referrals, etc. The second part entails filling in the content of the rows over time with specific strategies for each media type. For example, you find out about a charity event for mothers in your area, at the target age, income level, etc. that own homes. You would note "Clothing Recycle Charity May 25th" on your 10 x 10 in the column labeled "events". Now you have stored that potential strategy for future review in the second quarter of the year. Over time, the entire

10 x 10 becomes filled with strategies you've tested or strategies you would like to test in the future.

Another benefit of communicating with your targets in a 10 x 10  approach is getting the power of diversification. You are now using combinations to your advantage. Notice how unstable your marketing is when you only have one to three strategies producing the wealth of your new business. This means if you want to grow you would have to squeeze out more results from a limited number of areas or if one of the three strategies stopped working,  your business would decline significantly. Building into your business a 10 x 10 strategy approach means you will over time have ten different types of marketing working for you, rather than one to three. It also means that if you want to double your results – getting 100% improvement – rather than having to improve your two strategies by 50% you would only need to improve your ten strategies by how much? Only ten percent.

Something to notice is most businesses want more referrals. Why? Because they are easier to convert into long-term paying customers, they are ideal because they came highly recommended by an existing ideal client, and they are not concerned with price like other leads. If you agree that you would like to have more referrals in your business, than look back at your 10 x 10 and make sure one of your column labels is "referrals". This will force you to start learning, researching and looking for strategies to grow referrals. After all how many referral strategies are you allowed to have in business? Yes, unlimited. Even though there is no restriction to how many you are allowed to have in business – most businesses only have one to three. Imagine what your business will look like when you have ten or more.

Keep in mind while you are filling in your 10 x 10 playbook that marketing is not just about getting the first sale; it's also about getting them to come back and buy from you over and over again. We've already said many times that the targets you'll be identifying for your campaign could also be a customer that's already in your data base. If that's the case, you can also use the strategies in your 10 x 10 to go after the targets that fit. Always be thinking about marketing as a continuous process from the first sale to the last sale and how can you infuse the **5 Ways** strategies to grow profitable customers not just leads. For many  businesses,  you will have at least two to three target segments -  that means the owner must  go through this process of answering the 5 question campaign with 10 x 10 play sheets for each target segment. This is when *focus* becomes important in creating your future marketing strategy to grow your business.

## AIDA

There is a lot of research on what creates effective direct-sale marketing pieces – in other words selling from the page. Most small to medium business owners can't afford to do the brand awareness marketing of the large Coca Colas and Apples of the world. They need to actually get leads they can convert into customers from each and every possible marketing effort. In order to increase the likelihood of achieving direct-sale marketing results, you must understand how to use AIDA in every marketing piece from your website landing page, to your business cards, to your emails, and so on.

**A = Attention**
**I = Interest**
**D = Desire**
**A = Action**

# OMG! What's The Focus?

First part is *Attention* – why is it first? Because if you can't get your ideal target's attention then what's the point. The number one thing most marketing pieces have in common is the first thing you see is the business logo. Instead of putting a logo they don't yet recognize as your attention grabber, what if you used a powerful headline, an engaging image, or a call-out to the target themselves like "ATTENTION BUSY MOTHERS WHO OWN A HOME". Now you are using the prime real estate of the marketing piece to get their attention. In fact, your headline and engaging image should take up a minimum of 25% of the available space to be effective. Headlines should be a lead-in to have your target naturally continue reading like "Here's how you..." or "5 Reasons you..." so you can finish the story in the next parts.

The second part is all about creating *Interest*. This is where you use your USP, your benefits that matter most to your target, your guarantee – what is going to grab their interest in YOU.

The third part is *Desire* and the more desirable it is, the more likely they will make it to the fourth and final part. Desire is created through scarcity, gifts or content that create reciprocity, easy first step to test or trial, or an offer of something of actual value the target would have spent money or time on – use your offers here!

The last part is simple yet important – *Action*. What is your call to action? If you are not clear on what action you want them to take, then they will not be clear. Do you want them to visit a website, call a number, go to your social media page, hashtag a post, or walk into a store front? It is ok to have more than one contact listed but the action you want them to take should be the biggest, most obvious one. It should also be the one that you are prepared to have a process to capture the leads coming in through those calls, visits, posts, or click-through and convert them into customers.

## MARKETING CALENDAR

Once you have a campaign, your next concern is going to be where to *FOCUS* or where to start. This section is all about putting what you just outlined in your targeted marketing campaign(s) and 10 x 10 playbook(s) into a realistic format to use as a project management guide for the next 90 days. Some people prefer to look at the full 90 days, others prefer monthly.

To start you will need a table with 14 columns – the first left column is labeled "Strategy" and the additional 13 columns are labeled for the thirteen weeks in that quarter, for example "April 5-11", "April 12-18"...and so on. In the first column labeled "Strategy", enter the Target – Strategy you will be working on in the next quarter. For example, Mothers – Facebook Ads. You will continue to list all the Target-Strategy you will be using over the course of the next 13 weeks in the rows in the "Strategy" column. Then list out along each Target-Strategy row what small step you will take in each week. This will also allow you to move your *focus* around by looking at what weeks are busier than others. You're mapping out who you are targeting, and how you are going to do it. For example, your column with Mothers - Facebook Ads would have a first step that doesn't start until week three of the thirteen weeks which is "create 2 Facebook ad designs" and then in week five of the thirteen is "post ad 1 and set up targeting parameters" and so on.

Again, this allows you to do all the planning up front. Many businesses will want to hire other specialists or companies to help them get some leverage with different strategies. If you want to run an email campaign, for example, you might want to hire a graphic designer or a company that specializes in effective email marketing. When you plan ahead for these 90 days, you are setting the foundation for you to be as proactive as possible about timelines, deadlines, and priorities to manage yourself, your employees, and/or your outside vendors.

It's okay to make adjustments to the calendar or change different approaches as you go, but it's essential to make sure these changes are recorded on the calendar—especially if there are multiple people working on the campaigns. You should also be looking at your calendar every week to determine where you stand and what is coming up in the next week.

## MEASUREMENT

One last key step before you can start taking action on your 13-week plan for your *focused,* targeted marketing campaign(s) – how will you know if it worked or not? In a game of football, the only way you know if you are winning or losing is by looking at the scoreboard – and the only way to know if your marketing strategy is providing leads, customers, and profit is to know how you are measuring those key outcomes <u>before</u> any campaigns launch.

Right now your marketing dollars are recorded on your books as a fixed expense along with other typical business expenses like your rent, payroll, insurance or utilities. Although the difference between those expenses and your marketing expense is you actually expect something back from your marketing in the form of leads, customers, and profit. Now what if we called your marketing an investment instead of an expense? What do you automatically expect to get from an investment? Yes, a return. And how do you know if you're getting a return from an investment? Correct, you would measure it. See how this is working! Now, would you measure the overall return from all investments or would you measure how much you are getting from each individual investment you made? Each individual investment so you would know which one is yielding the best returns and which one needs traded (or eliminated from your portfolio of investments). The same is true for your marketing investments.  You will need to start measuring each strategy and what each one is returning for you.

**FREE RESOURCE DOWNLOAD**

Marketing Measurement Tool
www.actioncoachtampabay.com/measure

## UNLIMITED MARKETING BUDGET

There are two measurements you will need to know how to calculate to create an unlimited marketing budget: acquisition cost and lifetime value of a customer. The goal is to get the acquisition cost per customer as low as possible and to increase the value of your customers over the lifetime they are with you.

The first measurements you will need is your acquisition cost of a new lead and a new customer. This will be calculated by first collecting where do your clients hear about you so you know how many leads are coming in from each strategy. One way to make this even easier is to diversify your offers. That way when a lead redeems an offer or a code associated with an offer, you will know which strategy made them take action.

Acquisition cost is calculated by taking the total amount invested on a marketing strategy divided by how many leads that strategy created. The second step is to take the total amount invested and divide it by the number of new customers it created. For example, you invested $200 on Facebook Ads and that ad created 10 mothers to call and 2 of them became customers. That equates to an acquisition cost per lead of $20 ($200/10) and an acquisition cost per customer of $100 ($200/2). Now the fun part – answering the question did we make a return or not? To answer that question, all we need to know is how much revenue those two customers contributed – let's say $2,000 or $1,000 each – and how much of that revenue was profit? – let's say $1,000 or $500 each. That means you invested $100 for a customer that returned to you $400 in pure profit and $800 total profit return on your investment. If you gave a bank a one dollar bill and they gave you four dollars back – how many more times would you give the bank a dollar? Of course, over and over again. Well the same is true with the return on the example marketing strategy and you should run it over and over until it no longer delivers a profit. Many businesses stop running a campaign or a strategy – not because it stopped running a profit – but more likely because *they* got bored with it and wanted to try something more exciting. If you are going to try something more exciting – great! Just be sure that you get the strategy that is returning a profit to work like a machine with or without you there so it continues to run and you continue to see the score sheet to know it's returning a profit while you are off testing new, "more exciting" strategies.

Knowing these numbers also allows you to better plan and make better decisions. You can literally take the 13 week plan you just created and create a projected return based on goals for each strategy. In other words, if you know how much you are going to invest on a marketing strategy – for example a budget of $800 for Facebook Ads – then you can calculate how many leads and customers that strategy needs to produce to be profitable, right? By taking the average sale of $1,000 and average profit of $500 and dividing that into the total budget of $800. What do you get as a goal return on this example investment? You need one customer to produce a  revenue return ($200) and you will need two customers to produce a profit return ($200). That will allow you to determine whether or not this is a viable strategy to test or not. Let's say you found that you would need to get 1,000 new customers to make a profit – that might be higher than you think is achievable if your average return on strategies was 200 customers.

This level of decision making with measurement also allows you to proactively project what kind of response you will get and how you must plan to be ready to service and deliver consistently to that volume. Some strategies might bring you a hundred leads, in which you may need to hire more people to your team. Others might only give you one or two, but come with a great cash flow—meaning you have to commit a lot of cash in order to get that back and there might be some delay. Having the information about your needs for staff, service, supplies, or cash is extremely helpful in determining which strategies to implement and where to *focus* on a quarterly basis.

The other measurement to start paying attention to, in order to have an unlimited marketing budget, is your lifetime value. First you will need to know, on average, how long do your customer do business with you? Is it one month, six months, six years, twenty years? You will also need to know how much they spend on average when they buy from you. For example, the plumber knows that on average every new customer stays for an average of 30 months and spends on average $6,000 or $200 a month ($6,000/30=$200). That means each customer is worth $6,000 over their lifetime. But wait! What other value do your customers bring into your business? Referrals. What if you started measuring how many referrals your customers bring on average? By the way, do you think your referrals would go up or down if you started measuring them? The answer is always up. It is magical how something improves when you get focused on it and actually pay attention to its performance. Okay, let's factor in the value of referrals to our example: Let's say the average plumbing customer brings in 4 referrals at $6,000 each that is an additional $24,000 - bringing the grand total of lifetime value of one customer to $30,000. When you start calculating these numbers, it's always interesting to see how much value your customer is really bringing you. In some cases, you would probably stop treating each as a hundred dollar, one transaction client, and start looking at them like the 30 thousand dollar client they are. Again, with this information, you will make better decisions. If you have customers that represent thirty thousand dollars to you in the next 30 months –

would you say happy birthday? Would you send them a thank you card? Can you afford to send a $60 fruit arrangement for the holidays? It no longer becomes just about the first sale, it's about making sure that you boost every other sale from there on and what you are doing to move the number of referrals up.

## CHAPTER 5
## KEY THOUGHTS

◎ Definition of Marketing
◎ Unique Selling Proposition
◎ 5 Questions - Target Market Campaign
◎ 10 x 10 Playbook
◎ ROI Measurement
◎ AIDA

## OMG! WHAT'S THE FOCUS?
## ACTION STEPS

1) _____

2) _____

3) _____

4) _____

5) _____

## CONTINUED THINKING

◎ Guerrilla Marketing - Levinson
◎ Instant Leads – Sugars
◎ Purple Cow - Godin
◎ Instant Advertising – Sugars
◎ Buying Customers - Sugars

# 6

## Sales

*"No one wants to be sold but everyone wants to buy. There's no lotion or potion that will make sales faster and easier for you - unless your potion is hard work."* **– Jeffrey Gitomer**

Before we start talking about sales we need to first take a look at people's attitudes about sales. What are your beliefs about sales? This is an issue we face with business owners and teams all the time. Sales people have a pretty bad reputation, so many business owners are concerned about turning people away by being "too pushy and salesy." But the fact of the matter is that if we're not *focused on* sales, we're not going to have any business. Sales is the cornerstone of getting business and we're all involved in sales from the moment we get up in the morning; we're always selling our point of view to somebody. We're constantly trying to convince somebody to do something – for example trying to get our kids to get out of bed and get ready for school – that's all sales. Once we admit that, we can take advantage of it and improve not only our business, but our lives as well.

## THE IMPORTANCE OF TRAINING

One of the first things that all successful sales people have in common is that they're highly focused on training. You will not find a successful sales person who's not focused on training. We don't know any great sales professionals that want to act and behave like the classic used cars salesmen. No GOOD sales professionals are trying to trick you or lie and swindle you, or behave like some scam artist that's trying to sell you something you don't need. That's not what sales is about; sales is about professionally assisting people to make great buying decisions.

As you start thinking about what you want to be in sales, think about "ideal sales people" who have helped you in your life to make critically important decisions around some technology or some project that you didn't fully understand. Somebody that's taken time to explain things to you, has gone through the process with you and has helped you to make a great decision for yourself given your circumstances. If we're going to help more clients, we have to help them understand what it is that we can do for them if they purchase our service. Therefore, top performing sales professionals are first great

136

teachers and consultants about their category of products/solutions so they can tailor an approach to best meet customer needs. They help clients see their business or problem in a new way. Then assertively control the conversation to help the prospect make the best decision.

Even the most accomplished sales people, those who work for the top companies in the United States in sales, have training every week. They're constantly training, role playing, reading articles about sales and reading reviews with their mentors on which aspects of the products and services they are best at explaining. If you're going to be successful in your company in sales it's going to start with training -and a minimum of weekly training is critical. If you need a lot of improvement in sales results, you need to accelerate your sales training even more.

So really be thinking about what you could be doing every day to improve your skills in helping others better understand the value proposition of the products or services that you're bringing to the marketplace.

## THE RIGHT ATTITUDE

A lot of it is about your attitude. Really successful sales people are highly resilient, buoyant, and able to tolerate the ebbs and flows of their role in sales. Are you going to get turned down a lot in sales? Absolutely. You're going to approach people about your product and service and they're not going be interested. Overall there's a relatively small percentage of people; some people say as low as three percent of people that are actively considering your product category and are ready to buy your product today. And there's a much larger percentage of people who will never buy your product or service. But there's another percentage - somewhere around 10 percent - who would be willing to buy your product or service at some point. And some portion of them, if you explain the value of your product and service, and gave them a compelling reason to act would, in fact, be willing to buy today. That means if our whole target is maybe 10 to 15 percent of the target population that have the possibility of conversion, you're going to get a lot of no's before you get yes's.

One of the ways to reduce the no's is by targeting. If you do a great job at targeting prospects, automatically your conversion rate will go up because the people you're in front of will be more likely to be in the 10-15% who will buy your product or service at some point.

There's a great little book by Andrea Waltz and Richard Fenton *Go For No! Yes is the destination, No is how you get there!* The book tells a story that helps reiterate a great theory about how important it is to keep asking questions and going for no and being excited about getting a no. Because every time you get a no, guess what? You're one step closer to getting your next yes; the percentage of no's is going to be higher than the percentage of yes's. You have to be prepared to keep stepping up to bat if you're going to start getting a better average.

There are a couple of key things for high success in sales. First of all, it's an orientation of bringing value first. As Jeffrey Gitomer, the number one sales author of all time, says "Nobody wants to be sold, but everyone loves to buy!" It's not about you, it's about them. *Focus* on your target's needs, *focus* on what value you can bring to them. How can you help them see their business through a "new lens" based on your acquired knowledge of best practices.  Be clear on how you can help them improve efficiency, productivity and profit.  And once you find someone who truly needs your product or service, be relentless in your follow up until they go away or tell you to stop. Most initial "No's" are "No, not now" vs. "No, not ever" especially when you've determined that your product would be valuable to them.

If you're going to understand what they need and what value proposition would be exciting to them, is it about telling them or asking them? The obvious response is asking. We often tell our clients who we're coaching around sales that "questions are the answer" to a successful sales approach that is committed to bringing value in every interaction. The key is developing really great questions that are going to help you deeply understand the needs of your targeted population so that you can bring value to them. A sales process starts at the beginning, with the first contact that anybody has with your business. For example, if somebody calls your business, it's very common for them to ask the price of your product or service right off the bat. So right away, it could be easy to feel defensive. If you start by giving a price than the conversation will be about price and you will have failed in your commitment to *focus* on bringing value first and understanding the needs of the customer second. If you remain committed to an approach based on the premise that questions are the answer, what question could you ask to begin to understand what they really need?

For example, if somebody asks the price of a water heater, you could ask "Well just so I can help you best, may I ask you a few questions?" Their answers are always going to be something like, "Well, sure" or maybe guardedly, "OK". Now you can get more permission, and find out more information such as how many people they have living in the house, what they are looking for, whether or not they know what the differences are, etc. Are they interested in delivery and installation today? Is it an emergency? Is the permanent water heater leaking and creating a problem for them? Suddenly you're in a position where you're able to develop rapport and it's clear to the potential purchaser you care more about something than just throwing out a price; you're *focused* on what their needs are and meeting them.

# COMMUNICATION STYLES

The other thing is to become a student of understanding communication styles. This means learning about the communication styles of others, and how you can adjust your style to best meet the communication styles of others. Hard driving business owners, as one example, are frequently the purchasers of many services and want to get to the "bottom line" quickly. They're drivers, they want quick decisions and they want to decide so they will want a few options to choose from.  Engineers, on the other hand, are very detail-oriented. They're going to want a lot of information. They will study and think about the precise details from each angle before making a decision. So your approach to those two different types of potential customers needs to be customized to their individual needs and styles.

Start being a student of different communication styles and ways of noticing the differences early on so you can adjust your style. This is how people that are successful in sales dramatically improve their results. Again, there's an opportunity for preparation. What kind of a sales kit have you developed? What kinds of information do you have available? What is your process for researching the company? What are they going to find out about you? You do research on them to take a look at their company and learn information about who they are, what their competitors are, and you better believe or at least assume they're checking you out as well.

What do you look like on LinkedIn? What does your webpage look like – what are they going to learn about you and your style? It is important to manage your image because the first impressions that you leave with people, whether those are in person or online, really matter. It's what some people refer to as the "zero moment of truth". The first moment of truth is when you show up and they shake your hand and that's an opportunity for them to learn who you are; but frequently there's a zero moment of truth which is them checking you out on your website ahead of time, and you better believe they're looking at your Facebook and other social media pages as well. What does that look like if you're a sales professional? These are all things to keep in mind that can help increase your sales acumen and results dramatically.

## THE SALES PROCESS

As you develop your sales kit and discover what materials you're going to have with you, have a process that you're going to follow. What are the key things you want to make sure that you cover, and what are some options you have to present? Understanding and noticing what concerns or objections people give for not buying or delaying the decision is very important. The same objections will usually be raised consistently so once you know them, you have a better chance of anticipating and getting out ahead of them. There are a lot of things that you can anticipate and, certainly once you get into the field of sales, start writing down and noticing the specific objections that prospects raise, and then in the future, bring them up earlier in the process. For example, you've frequently gotten push back about the delay between contract execution and the implementation start date for your services. So early in your face-to-face with qualified prospects you say: "I have occasionally been asked about the very deliberate process we follow prior to implementation, would it be ok if I spent a few minutes to explain why we do that for your preparation and long term satisfaction?"

Don't be in a position as a sales person where you're sort of saying to yourself, "Oh, I hope he doesn't bring up the question about price." Then if they do, you're going to react defensive rather than proactive.

**FREE RESOURCE DOWNLOAD**

Objections Exercise
www.actioncoachtampabay.com/object

In sales, once you have a qualified lead it is critical to think about creating rapport. Being genuine and truly focusing on being positive, fun and authentic are key. Referrals are great because they have a very high conversion rate. The reason they have such a high conversion rate is because a lot of the risk questions in every prospect's mind have already been asked and answered before they get in contact with you. And they were answered by someone with some first-hand knowledge of you and your products. Consider how you can replicate this in your sales process.

The sales process starts with getting a call or a lead into the business, but what's the next step? Until the person is turned into a closed sale, how could you be creating rapport all along the way? What are ways to create confidence, share testimonials and results, or other pieces of critical information with the prospect throughout the process so that when they actually sit down with you, they feel like they were a referral to your business?

Look at how you're quoting, how you're unique, and what the unique selling points of doing business with you are. Another big part of creating rapport, as we've mentioned earlier is understanding prospect's different communication styles.

# DISC PROFILE

In working with Dr. Tony Alessandra, Hall-of-Fame Keynote Speaker and author of *The Platinum Rule for Small Business Success,* we have developed a deep understanding and a comprehensive array of offerings with the DISC assessments. The DISC assessment measures four distinctive behavioral characteristics called D-I-S-C: **Dominance, Influence**, **Steadiness** (and patience), and **Conscientiousness** (compliance and structure). We use DISC evaluations and training to assist our business owners, executives and sales professionals by increasing their self-awareness and the opportunity for self-management for improved emotional intelligence and ultimately sales success.

1. **Dominant.** As we mentioned earlier, most are decision makers and about fourteen percent of the general population are predominantly "D" personality types. "D"s need to feel in control, they like to make decisions, and to quickly get to a few options. They are dominant. If you're working in a sales process with them you need to have your information really tight and be able to present it to them in a very short period of time. When you're in their office they may tell you they only have 15 minutes. If they do, that is when you respond, "That's fine. I'll only need five." Make sure you stick to the 5 minutes.

2. **Influencers.** For "I"s, it's really important who they know and connecting you to who they know. They often have very coordinated clothing and they have a large group of friends around them. If you're ever having a party they're great people to help organize it. When you meet with them you'll go into their office and notice everything about their lives. Make sure you pay attention and compliment them on their latest award or vacation experience.  They often smile with their eyes. Spending time on rapport building with "I's" will be critical to success. They have to like you first – think relationship.

3. **Steadfast.** They're the people that hold the organization together. They're the ones that are the planners.  They are the ones who really want to know the beginning to the end. Make sure you provide that for them throughout the sales process. You'll often have to provide more information in a sequential manner because it's important for them to see the whole picture. They really want to understand so they can do the very best for you or their company. Think pleasers.

4. **Conscientious.** When it comes to the "C" group, these are the people who are the detail-oriented thinkers. They like to come up with solutions that are precise and measurable. They need even more information than the S's because they want to understand all of the details in order to  make those decisions. If you regularly interact with CFO's, CPA's or engineers, you know what we mean. Think precise.

When it comes to the sales process, you will not have someone who is specifically one trait, but rather a combination.

That's okay. The goal is to identify their predominant trait so you know how to speak their language to connect and better meet their needs. It makes a tremendous impact in your results when you *focus* on them.

Many times you can actually tell who you're talking to on the phone just by the volume of their voice. A lot of times the D's and I's are much more outgoing, so their voices will be higher, strong in volume, and they will speak quickly. The S's and the C's will talk a lot slower and quieter so expect periods of silence in the conversation.

**FREE RESOURCE DOWNLOAD**
Quick DISC Quiz
www.actioncoachtampabay.com/disc

Then there is also another helpful tool called **VAK** (**V**isual **A**uditory and **K**inesthetic) which relates to the individual's learning or information processing styles. Most people in the population are visual and kinesthetic (they need to touch and interact with the environment), and then thirdly auditory. So in presenting information, make sure you have something visual because it will paint a picture for the prospect (visual) and if possible, something for prospects to touch and hold. Storytelling and parables that relate to your product or service has also been shown to be a very successful tool because it verbally paints a picture in the prospects mind of how your product "works".

The arguments you may hear from visual people are that they can't visualize something you are talking about, or they prefer to see a diagram of something you are trying to explain. Kinesthetic people might use language like "I can't wrap my hands around it". Auditory people will say they are listening for the main event, or what you are saying just isn't resonating with them. If you apply strategies for each type of learner into your sales cycle, you can offer a fuller array of options to meet individual needs and will get better results.

## WHY WOULD YOU DO ASSESSMENTS LIKE DISC?

Seven reasons why you would use assessments:

1. Improve Hiring and Selection
2. Increase Sales
3. Improve Customer Service
4. Increase Productivity
5. Reduce Employee Turnover
6. Customize Employee Training
7. Model Team Building

For more detailed explanation of these seven reasons why you would use assessments in your business, please go to http://www.actioncoachtampabay.com/services/assessments/

## CHAPTER 6
## KEY THOUGHTS

◎ Importance of Training
◎ Sales Attitude
◎ Communication Styles
◎ Sales Process
◎ DiSC

## OMG! WHAT'S THE FOCUS?
## ACTION STEPS

1) _____

2) _____

3) _____

4) _____

5) _____

## CONTINUED THINKING

◎ Instant Sales – Sugars
◎ Little Gold Book of YES! Attitude – Gitomer
◎ Go for No – Waltz and Fenton
◎ Little Red Book of Selling – Gitomer
◎ The Platinum Rule – Dr. Alessandra

# 7

# Systems

*"SYSTEM stands for Save Yourself Time, Energy and Money ... create a system every week and eventually you won't have to work, your business will work so you don't have to ..."* – **Brad Sugars**

This is where we start the process of getting the business to work without the owner. By systemizing each section of how the business runs, from how the phone is answered to how the management team performs activities, planning, and strategy, we look at how we can simplify and systemize the business to enable both consistency and predictability.

There are four key areas for creating systems.

## 4 Components of Systemization

| | |
|---|---|
| **Systems & Technology**<br>Documenting and automating your business so it works without you predictably every time! | **Delivery & Distribution**<br>Get it on time to the right place – the 1st time and Every time. Consistency & Efficiency. |
| **Accounting, Test & Measure**<br>Know the numbers from both the Marketing & Cash point of view. Key Performance Indicators. | **People & Education**<br>Recruit them WELL. Treat them WELL. Train them and help them perform an amazing job. |

Systemizing your business will mean it will operate in a predictable fashion even when you're not there!

1. **Delivery and Distribution.** This goes back to our conversation about the mastery level of success, clarifying how the system is delivering every single time. The key to great service and repeat customers is consistency and meeting commitments

2. **People and Education.** What do you have in place to train your team? How can you educate them? Can they work autonomously? Training is critical in improvement and success. Is there a consistent system for "on-boarding" new team members? Does everyone have a job description? What is the system for recognition and reward?

3. **Accounting, Measure and Test.** Look at the different areas in your business. If you had a series of Key Predictive Indicators (KPIs) and accrual-based accounting reports, you could manage

your business better - driving it forward with proper measuring and testing. We've talked about this before in the 5 ways and in the key indicators as well as in the marketing chapter.

4. **Systems and Technology.** Where does your business lack in structure? Where do you lack technology, automation, speed, knowledge, etc.? It could be simple, like storing the passwords used in the business in one secure location. How are you completing & documenting routine maintenance? How are you regularly backing up important files and checking security of your systems?

In each of the 4-ways for creating systems in your business, there are numerous ways for developing systems in each business. For a list of 83 ideas for systems development, to get you started, download "4-ways of Systems List Tool to begin creating your own list. We challenge you to do the exercise.

**FREE RESOURCE DOWNLOAD**

4 Areas of Systems List Tool
www.actioncoachtampabay.com/four

## SYSTEMS CREATE LEVERAGE

We've mentioned leverage in earlier chapters. There are three different definitions that sum up what "leverage" means in this context. We often ask business owners for examples of leverage. Some say a wheelbarrow because you couldn't lift the dirt if you didn't have the power of leverage the wheelbarrow provides. Same with a car jack, you couldn't lift a car without the leverage of the jack to change a tire.

The first definition: Leverage is doing evermore with ever less. Developing and training your team to use systems will allow you to do more in your business with less time, less sweat and less money.

The second definition:  Leverage is dividing to multiply.  What areas can you divide into simple steps? What from those steps can you improve to multiply the overall system results? Think of the 5 Ways. To multiply profitability, you divided it down into five different areas, then improved each step by only 10% to garner a 61% increase in profit. Work easier for higher results.

The last definition: Leverage is doing things once and getting paid forever (or at least for a long time).  If you don't document your processes, you are destined to repeat those actions (or instructions to your team) over and over again. But when you write things down, you receive a return in the long run. For example, if you wrote a script on how to get the best returns on phone calls, those written instructions will pay you on and on. Other aspiring business owners might want to purchase your system.

Here's another example of a system mastered by monkeys. Most people peel bananas the same way – starting at the top with the stem. Some struggle, biting the bended top to peel it back. Well, monkeys, who have opened way more bananas than most humans, have their own faster, more efficient system. Simply flip the banana upside down—that's right, not the stem side, the end side—and pinch the tip. Notice how it pops open without any struggle?  It's a simple system and we'll bet you'll never open a banana the old, harder way again – right?

## HOW TO WRITE A SYSTEM

Before you can start writing a systems, first you must step back and look at the bigger picture to research, discover, create, or recover the rules and policies that impact the very system you are setting out to write. These rules or policies can be in the form of company culture points, owner's values, company vision, government regulations and legislation, industry standards and restrictions, your marketing and USP, your sales, your team, your operation, and any other rules involved in shaping "how things are done around here". Once you have a list of those and you think you have most of them, then you are ready to move on to method. A shortcut tip is to write out the "job description" or total responsibilities for the part of the business, individual or department, in charge of executing that system – and that will give you a great outline to help you think of rules and policies as well as methods which is coming up in the next step.

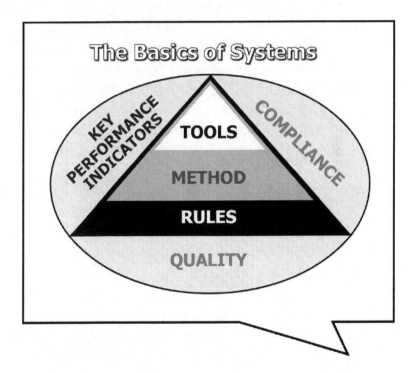

The next step involves recording the method in which you complete the system from start to finish. Method includes two parts: the process and the procedure. The process is a set of logically related tasks performed to achieve defined outcomes. It sets out to describe how the company will translate the rules or policy into action with a visual map or flowchart. Now, outline section by section how your business processes work. Begin your process by identifying the starting point of the system and the ending point that signifies it is complete. Take for example the process for depositing a check payment. The starting point is receiving a customer's check payment in the mail and the end point is that it was deposited at the bank. The process includes multiple steps in between those two points like receive check, enter into QuickBooks, sign back of check, complete deposit form, and take to the bank as a deposit. This example process has one step that involves multiple steps and therefore needs a written procedure for that step. A procedure provides detailed instructions to ensure that tasks in the process can be repeated with the same outcome every time by different people. Have you guessed which step in the example needs a procedure yet? Right, entering the check deposit into QuickBooks. As you saw in the financial chapter, there are two very different ways of accounting accrual and cash so that means one person could potentially "enter a check into QuickBooks" very differently from another person without having a detailed procedure on how it should be done to get consistency. Many times procedures are enhanced through the use of screenshots, video demonstrations, examples, or tools which just so happens to be the next step in creating a system.

Tools are also sometimes called props and can be in the form of software, forms, templates, videos, automation, standard documents, labels, notices, folders, guidebooks, checklists and signs. The last part of the overview involves the tools. When you are writing your procedures and processes, keep asking yourself what tool would make it easier to consistently complete this method over and over again? A common tool that is used in businesses today is default email. If you have answered a commonly asked question once in an email, then you can save that email as a tool for others to work from over and over rather than always creating one from scratch to end up answering the same question in different ways.

This word consistency leads perfectly into the fourth part of creating systems which is compliance or quality control. It is all about identifying policies, tasks in the process, procedures, and/or tools that have a big negative impact on compliance and ultimately the control of quality outcomes. The best way to identify these impact points is to uncover who are the end users and what do they see as measures of success and high quality outcomes? Armed with that information you can look over the process and procedures you just created, ask yourself on a scale of one to ten (ten being the highest), what task when performed inconsistently has the biggest negative impact on delivering the quality desired outcome? In other words, where are the bottlenecks, potential areas for delays, common mistakes or complaints that could keep this system from running at a high quality level? It is also important to understand that compliance and quality levels will very much depend on the expectations of the end users and your governing policies. For example, the compliance level for surgeons dealing with life or death procedures might be different than your postman delivering your mail on time, late, or not at all. You have to decide what your level of compliance will be and set key performance indicators to monitor your ability to consistently hit that standard.

Perfect transition for the last but not least step of creating a system – setting  key performance indicators or KPIs for short. KPIs are used to identify key areas and develop a set of measureable indicators of performance for each quality control task, position, team, manager or company to better predict in a shorter amount of time how well that level of compliance is being reached. It also makes it crystal clear for the employee or department running that system what points of that process are most crucial to focus on – and brings that same clarity for new or onboarding employees right away. That means whether someone is out on sick leave, quits suddenly or simply took their eye off the ball, leadership and management will have a regularly reported number that will tell them quality is slipping before it has slipped, fallen, and can't get customers back up.

Quick exercise: Start simple by writing a list of items for which you know you are inefficient because they commonly have to be re-done, re-educated, re-delegated, and/or regularly cause duplicated work. Then identify tasks that are done on a daily basis making them very redundant and showing a small efficiency would have a powerful compounding effect every day thereafter.  For example, most of us have multiple sign-ins and passwords which causes the need to reset forgotten passwords. What if you took thirty minutes to store all of the links, user names, emails, and passwords of every sign-on you use in one password-protected excel spreadsheet? How much time would that save you a month from now? A year from now? Wow. You are probably starting to notice how much money is truly wasted in inefficient tasks. As Darren Hardy said in *The Compound Effect,* the little things compound into huge results. Start with the little inefficiencies and you will find your system will compound into an overall efficient system. As Brad Sugars would say, "If you do something more than once without writing it down, then you are destined to do it forever." Write it down and systemize it so you aren't doing it forever.  You will be happy that you did when you bring a new employee on and the system is already documented!

Start from a higher perspective by using your organizational chart. Typically, there's a top end owner, general manager, and key areas in the business, including administration, sales, marketing, operations, finance, and human resources. Write out each position. Write the rules under each department. Under marketing, is there an intern, or an assistant? Then write job descriptions and manuals for each position. If you are planning on expanding your employee base, you may also want to have an ready-made ad to match the behavioral characteristics you are looking for in each position.  Ask the tough questions. Remember you are looking for a great match for your team.

# SAMPLE SALES SYSTEM
# SYSTEM-001

## 16 STEP SALES SYSTEM
PURPOSE OF THIS SYSTEM:
TO SYSTEMATICALLY GET NEW CLIENTS

1. Identify Business Development Opportunity (a lead)
2. Research the company / industry (Internet)
3. Set appointment – *Script #A*
   a. Referral   b. New Prospect
4. Send thank you email – *Script #B*
5. Day of meeting call – *Script #C*
6. Rapport meeting #1 – *Script- #D*
7. Thank you call – *Script #E*
   a. (Set next appointment)
8. Send follow-up hand written note – *Script #F*
9. Follow up 30 day call, -*Script #G*
   a. for existing clients
10. Call to schedule Meeting #2 – *Script #H*
11. Send confirming email or phone call
    *(similar to *Script #B)*
12. Call on "day of" meting – (similar to *Script #C*)
13. Conduct meeting #2 – *Script #I*
14. Position for referrals – *Script #J*
15. Send Manager thank you card –
    *(similar to Script #F)*
16. Manager 30 Day Follow Up – *Script #K*

*Sample-Sixteen step sales system*
*Date Last Revised: 1/31/2015*

## CHAPTER 7
## KEY THOUGHTS

- ◎ 4 Components of Systemization
- ◎ 3 Types of Leverage
- ◎ Four Areas of the Business
- ◎ How to Write a System
- ◎ Quality Outcomes and Accountability

## OMG! WHAT'S THE FOCUS?
## ACTION STEPS

1) _____

2) _____

3) _____

4) _____

5) _____

## CONTINUED
## THINKING

- ◎ Instant Systems - Sugars
- ◎ Instant Scripts Ebook - Sugars
- ◎ Instant Testing & Measuring Ebook - Sugars
- ◎ Six Sigma for Dummies - Gygi, DeCarlo, and Williams
- ◎ E-Myth Revisited - Gerber

# 8

## Team

*"If you want to grow a great company, grow some great people … build a training program for each and every one of them, specific to them, so they can become the best employee possible. If you train your employees, some may leave … but if you don't train them, they will all stay." –* **Brad Sugars**

When you are creating a team, you obviously want to make sure it is going to be a great one. Most businesses hire when they are desperate to fill a position so the process of recruitment is fast. The challenge of hiring quickly with little assessment of overall fit for the position is then compounded by the fact that most businesses fire very slowly leaving an employee in a position for far too long. When the most effective way to grow an all-star team is the complete opposite: always be recruiting, hire slowly and take extra steps to ensure fit for the position, and fire or switch roles faster if the goals are not achieved. Most businesses have the same recruitment process: create an ad based on the position and experience needed, then post it in various places. Then they read the resumes they get and narrow them down to the people they want to interview. They conduct interviews and background checks, call references (occasionally but only the ones listed on the resume) and then they're done. They decide from there which candidate they are going to hire. The problem is, studies show that this process only achieves about a 27% statistical probability of hiring someone who is a match for the position—which means the chances are they will not perform well and won't stay to work for you for a long period of time (or worse, might stay but remain disengaged). Many businesses have first year employee turnover of 50% or more. Ouch!

Fortunately there is a recruitment process that takes advantage  of what has been shown to statistically work to create better job matching. By going well beyond the traditional means of interviewing, background checking and reference processing, you can actually achieve an 85% statistical probability of hiring someone who is a match for your position.  When you add in the *Score Card* method described in the book *Who* by Geoff Smart and Randy Street you will have the added benefit of starting your process with amazing clarity and *focus* about who you are really looking for in an "A" player for your organization.

## FOUR  HOUR RECRUITMENT PROCESS

First, you need to figure out who is the best target for the position. What is their communication style? Are they a driver or an influencer? Are they steady or calculating? Once you have started to figure out the answers to these types of questions, you can place an ad on what would they actually care about in the job and why they should choose you, and eventually you can figure out how and where to communicate with them.

As you begin to think about the characteristics of your "A" player, you will want to develop a *Score Card* for each of the positions you are looking for. Having the focus and clarity to make sure that you are recruiting the person for the right purpose is key. The scorecard is composed of three parts. The Score Card begins with the job's mission – its overall purpose. Next, it defines the objective outcomes that the person in the position must produce in the next 12-24 months. And finally, it lists the competencies (the behavioral characteristics) that are critical for the individual to be successful and to fit within the team and culture of the organization. *Focus* on the specialist not the generalist so that you will have the competence you are looking for in the position.

Most people get hired based on experience, but they get fired based on attitude. More businesses should use that lesson to hire based on soft skills and communication styles rather than just experience. Experience and skill should be secondary. If they meet the basic requirements and have the perfect mind set and attitude, your training process can help get them up to speed if they lack experience.

The second point of the four hour recruiting process is based on saving you time by letting the candidate deselect themselves for you. This will keep you from having to go through hundreds and hundreds of resumes, which we all know is a tedious task that we all wish we could avoid. Allow the candidates to deselect themselves by setting up a designated phone number so they can call in and answer a series of two or three questions on a voice mail recording as well as electronically submit their resume to a given location. This can be done with a free Google Voice line. This allows you to see who is confident and serious enough to not only call, but also to leave a message articulating their response to the questions. This process will deselect all those who are applying for any and all positions. It also tends to rise to the top those who are seriously interested in your position. You can hear their voice, how they express themselves, and how quickly they can get to the point. This process will also show you who will follow the directions or not.

You can then choose from the candidates you like best and who you would like to invite to the group interview —the third point of the system. The group interview seems a little odd to business owners who haven't been exposed to this approach, but it is actually kind of a magical thing to see. Imagine inviting ten to fifteen people to a group interview and having some not show up on time. Obviously, they would be weeded out from the group of candidates. On the other hand, when it is a one on one and the candidate is a bit late, you'll be more likely to excuse it and conduct the interview anyway, whenever they do arrive. If they are late at the interview, they will most likely be late for work later. Would this be someone that would fit in a highly productive team?

In the group interview you should first talk about the position, what your company is about and then determine if they are still interested in applying. This is a great time to take a short break and invite those that are still interested to stay for the second part. If some candidates are no longer interested, great! They are welcome to deselect themselves and leave at that point. After the break, the table turns and you get to ask them questions in front of their competition. You can imagine that the applicants now try to *win* the position. The applicants are seeing how many talented people are competing for this same position and it becomes something they are motivated to win, rather than just be given out of desperation to fill a vacancy. At the end of the group interview, they can decide to either apply for the position, or again, deselect themselves. The team members you invited to participate always have great insights about the candidates to share and they now feel engaged in the selection process.

We assisted a CEO of a small insurance company in this process of recruiting and not only were we surprised how few people came appropriately dressed for this outside sales position but also that they all stayed after the break! When we came back into the room after the break, you could have cut the tension in the air with a knife. Ultimately, the CEO did not select any of the applicants in that round even though they all thought they were deserving. The CEO saved hours of one on one interviewing and was able to adjust his process to attract a better candidate pool.

Remember there are several points in this four point system that allow them to deselect. Zappos has a brilliant method of recruiting; they actually offer a thousand dollars to anyone who is willing to walk away from the position at the very end before the decision to hire is made. This is done to save the company the expense of anyone who is not truly committed to the vision, mission, culture and goals of Zappos. The money is offered to see if they will take the money and walk away or reveal their motivation and commitment to the team.

Next, once you've had a group interview and have candidates who want to continue; you invite only the top prospects for a one on one interview. Once they come back for the one on one interview, anyone who is selected from that interview will stay for skills testing and behavioral communication assessment. We provide all assistance with this hiring process, including a wide range of assessments which have different purposes for what you are screening. We can also help with the skills testing. This step is so important because you will be able to tell if this person is going to be up to speed and able to handle the responsibilities of the job within minutes. It also allows for them to see whether or not this is something they could picture themselves doing day in and day out. In our experience, there is such a gap in professionals that claim to be highly skilled, for example in book keeping but are unable to pass a basic accounting skills test. Make sure you are really paying attention to the candidates you are attracting.

Usually by the end of this process, you've got one or two potential employees that are excited to win the job, want to be a part of your team, and are ready to roll at the speed you need them to. At that point, it's about how well your onboarding, training and employee engagement process performs to keep them for a lifetime.

When it comes to recruiting top performing employees to your team, you need to keep them involved and engaged in a way that relates to long term retention. Every small business knows that turnover in a business costs too much lost productivity, time and resources and it's something to continuously work to reduce. Ask yourself, what really engages different employees?

## EMPLOYEE ENGAGEMENT

Looking at statistics around engagement, one of the top global consultants in human resources found that only 21% of the employees were engaged. An engaged employee readily gives of their voluntary and discretionary effort. And 41% are what they call "enrolled"— meaning the worker was capable, they cared about the organization and were ready to be engaged. But, alarmingly, 38% of the employees were disengaged. This worker has basically no positive connection to the organization and no intention of changing. That's pretty frightening when you think about the impact of only 62% of the employee base of those companies being either enrolled or engaged.

What are the drivers for engagement in a company? What things can you do to really enhance engagement? Actually, the good news is that there are some great resources around this. The key to engagement is well documented by Towers and Perrin, and by the Gallup Organization who has data from ten million employee satisfaction surveys globally. Their research has led to understanding which of the employee satisfaction survey questions which are answered positively correlate to highly successful companies or units inside of larger companies.

Based on the Towers and Perrin's research, which is very similar to the results from the Gallup research, there are five things in the United States that are the key drivers to engagement.

1. **Senior management is sincerely interested in employee wellbeing.** If you want to have employee engagement, then the employees have to feel that the senior management of the company really cares.

2. **Employees feel that they improved their skills and capabilities over the prior year.** It turns out that, not too surprisingly, that people are really driven and excited when they feel like they are learning and developing—when they are mastering new skills and developing as individuals. Companies that provide opportunities for employees to grow and develop actually really reap the rewards.

3. **The organization has a reputation for social responsibility**. People want to work for a company that's ethical, doing the right thing, and working on ways to help the community that they're in. Another way to engage your community and, at the

same time, employees is to be involved in things that demonstrate your social responsibility.

4. **Employees feel that they input into some decision making in their department**. Building mechanisms for employees to be involved in decision making and to be included is critical for them to feel that they're engaged.

5. **Employees feel the organization quickly resolves customers concerns.** This one may not be as obvious as some of the others. But employees really want to work for a company that they feel is, again, doing the right thing. When they are, employees respond by being more loyal, willing to work harder and giving of their voluntary and discretionary effort to the company.

Many companies are looking to improve engagement because it has a huge return on investment. One study by McKinsey and Company found that high performers generate up to 29% higher revenue than average performers. Therefore, getting engagement up makes a big difference. The companies in another study by Towers and Perrin found that companies with high employee engagement had a 19% increase in operating income and almost a 28% growth in earnings per share. Conversely, companies with low levels of engagement saw their operating income drop by more than 32% and earnings per share decline by 11%. Employee engagement is something that a lot of people are talking about right now. In our coaching practice, we work with a number of companies around employee engagement. We have great tools for measuring and comparing it to national norms. We have great systems and tools for helping leaders build their performance around employee engagement and developing a more positive culture in a company.

Now that we have talked about how to recruit the A player and engage them, let's talk about how we build a strong team. We see this as a great opportunity to have a smooth-running company. Unfortunately, in most businesses these tenants are often missed or absent. Having the *focus* on these six keys will lead your company to success!

# 6 KEYS TO BUILDING A WINNING TEAM

1.  **Strong Leadership**: Leaders think about the future and help others see the future. They are committed to growing individuals and organizational capability and they are actively looking for ideas to improve and then champion the ideas in the organization. Many owners concentrate on the technical side of business, being busy doing the work and meeting deadlines. To develop and grow they must be able to delegate more so they can work ON the business rather than IN the business.

2.  **Common Goal**: Making sure every single person in the business understands and can articulate the common goals of the business.

3.  **Rules of the Game**: All team members must know the rules and they must be written down and readily available. By having these defined and written by the business owner it gives a greater understanding to existing team members as well as new team members as to what is acceptable behavior and what is not. These rules will form the basis of the company culture - as long as they obey these rules they have the freedom to develop the business.

4.  **Action Plan**: Creating an action plan and making sure that managers in every single department understand it and how it relates to specific business areas is key.

5.  **Support Risk Taking**: If the leader does not take risks, then the

team will not push the boundaries.  All business need innovations to grow. Supporting people to take new strides, find more ways to be efficient, build new relationships and create new ways of doing things is critically important.

6. **100% Inclusion and Involvement:** How are you getting every single employee to understand their role and the impact they have on the overall success of the team? Engaging employees and including their ideas for improvement encourages ownership.

To learn more about how to arrange for an employee engagement survey for your team to benchmark against national averages, go to http://www.actioncoachtampabay.com/services/assessments/employee-engagement-assessments/

## "FORK IN THE ROAD" EMPLOYEE TERMINATION SYSTEM

Despite our best efforts at recruiting and leading, there are times when the business leader must make the often difficult decision to terminate and employee.  This decision is often delayed unnecessarily because the conversation is difficult and the individual has not done anything blatant to violate the rules of conduct.  When it's obvious that an employee is not performing to expectations and all efforts have been made to assist them, the ideal method is the "Fork in the Road".

This is a technique for terminating an employee when the primary issue is related to their performance in the job. This is not for someone who has overtly broken rules like stealing, failure to report for duty, sexual harassment, fighting or any other gross negligence or misconduct. This is for employees who are making a good effort but are not working out (delivering the desired results).

**Basic Script:**

Maintain a calm and warm demeanor.  Do not engage in debate or defending your position if possible.  Your position is that they are a "good person" but you have lost confidence in their ability to be successful here and at this time.  You sit down with the employee one on one and say:

- "First of all I want to say that I really appreciate your loyalty up to this point, and … <provide any other positive praise for the individual as a person and their efforts performance for a few minutes>".

- "Despite all of the things I like about you as an individual, we've unfortunately reached a fork in the road.  I've *lost confidence* in your ability to be successful in this role." (The phrase "I've lost confidence in you" is key to this process working so it needs repeated at least three times.)

- "Since I've lost confidence, if we continue down the road of your continued employment, I'm concerned that it will lead to you being terminated for cause.  If you decide to stay, I'll have to begin (or continue) to document everything that I feel have been performance issues, we will have to jointly develop a very tight performance improvement plan.  Even with these efforts, since *I've lost confidence* in your ability to be successful, I think this path will still lead to your termination for cause.  I respect you as an individual and know you've made efforts to do a good job so I would rather that not happen.  It is always challenging to have to explain a termination form employment when seeking your next position."

- "The alternative – the other fork in the road is that you could decide to resign.  If you were to voluntarily resign, I am prepared to do a variety of things to assist you in your transition to another position.  I would be willing to: ... "

- o "agree to give neutral or positive references to future employers focused on what you did great." and

- o "support any reasonable "story" as to you reason for leaving to all outside inquires."

- o "support your "story" here as well and will not tell any other story to the rest of the team as to your reasons for resigning."

- o "provide extra pay to assist you in transition <Give something more than you are required to do like 1-2 weeks of pay for transition>"

- o Option: "we will not dispute a claim for unemployment if you file one."

- o Option:  If they would normally be required to give a notice for resignation (such as 2 weeks), you might decide to give them the option of not working during the notice period or deciding you don't want them to work (but pay them)

- "In exchange for all of that, I will want you to agree to sign a release saying that you will not talk bad about us in the community, you will not attempt to take any of our business (clients) or recruit any other employees, you will not make any claims about being terminated unfairly and that you have received your full pay while you have been in our employment (option: and you are stating will not make a claim for unemployment)." *(Note: we have sample agreements)*

- "I encourage you to take the release with you to review it and to have your attorney review it as well if you desire. I encourage you to consider your options carefully and return to me with your answer no later than... <set a specific date and time within 2-3 days>."

*NOTE: Never do this on a Friday – schedule the 1st meeting earlier in the week so they can ask questions during the week. Give a deadline of an answer of a few days (for example, if it is a Monday – give until Thursday at the latest).*

- "You may take until <whatever day you stated earlier> to decide but I would encourage you to take the resignation package I've given you so that I can openly assist you in getting settled in your next position. In the interim, call me or email me if you have any questions."

*NOTE: Important to not get into a debate about who did what or who else might be to blame. Focus on respecting them as an individual and protecting their dignity. Phrases such as "You're a good person and I'm sure you will do well somewhere else. I've just lost confidence in you for this position but I'm sure you will be great somewhere else." Blame, excuses, anger - respond with something like: "I get it and I know you try hard – I've lost confidence in your ability in this position. Just keep repeating that.*

This system works well because confidence is not something that they can debate because you already said how great they are and how much they have tried. You are simply saying you have lost confidence which is acknowledging and stating an insight about your view and not about them personally.

## CHAPTER 8
## KEY THOUGHTS

- Employee Scorecard
- 4 Point Recruitment Process
- Employee Engagement
- 6 Keys to a Winning Team
- Fork in the Road

## OMG! WHAT'S THE FOCUS?
## ACTION STEPS

1) _____
2) _____
3) _____
4) _____
5) _____

## CONTINUED THINKING

- Instant Team Building - Sugars
- Who - Smart and Street
- First Break All The Rules – Buckingham
- Gung Ho – Blanchard
- Speed of Trust – Covey
- What Got You Here Won't Get You There - Goldsmith

# 9

## Planning

*"That's been one of my mantras - focus and simplicity. Simple can be harder than complex: You have to work hard to get your thinking clean to make it simple. But it's worth it in the end because once you get there, you can move mountains."* - **Steve Jobs**

This is the chapter where you will learn how to "pull it all together" into a *FOCUSED* plan of attack so you leave this book with a plan to keep your eye on driving towards your future goals and objectives. At this point you've already thought about the attitude and mindset it's going to take to achieve change and really implement new thinking in order to get new results. You've also realized where you are going, where you want to be in the future, what you really want to accomplish, and what it's going to take to create a business that could work without you. You're starting to realize how you are spending your time and how you can re-invest it into driving the business forward. You've also realized where you financially need to grow some strength and how you can start looking at your finances with the future in mind. You've learned about your marketing, how to set up campaigns and put them into a marketing calendar. You've learned about sales and how to improve your conversion rate through your team and communication styles. You've learned how to identify areas and systems that you can take on in the next 90 days that will give you some easy return on your payroll on a daily or weekly basis. You've learned how to build a team, how to recruit them and how to get them more engaged so they are giving you more voluntary and discretionary effort. Now it's time to pull all of those lessons together into a highly focused ONE page plan that includes your annual goals, next quarter goals and what you will be working on in the next week or two weeks that is directly linked to moving you towards your 90 day goals.

## SEQUENCE OF A PLAN

Finally, you are ready to write a plan! You have been learning, writing, and reading all of the core elements you will need to create a powerful plan to achieve the successful action you are out to obtain.

Here are the five core elements that when used to your advantage you will see a multiplied effect on your results:

**DREAM**

**X**

**GOAL**

**X**

**LEARN**

**X**

**PLAN**

**X**

**ACTION**

The first element is a DREAM, which you already explored in the beginning of this book. Without a clear dream and vision in mind then it will be difficult to set goals for tremendous growth. The second element is GOAL which is a key component to you moving your dreams forward. Without a goal those dreams just become wishes. You have been working on many examples of goal setting in this book from your time, team, marketing, sales, and financials. The third element is LEARN and oh this is an important one. In fact, most go from goal straight to plan without even stopping to learn first. Fortunately for you, this book has been providing you with a massive amount of information, how-to's and best practices to help you with any aspect of your plan. Plus you are now connected to a wealth of resources and support through your coaching team at ActionCOACH Tampa Bay. Why is the LEARN element so important? Because you could literally take a goal and write a plan that will take you to actions that are not going to get you the result you want in the most efficient and effective manner. It is in the learning about how to achieve your goals that the plan should be formulated and the strategies should be outlined. The fourth element is PLAN and this is right where we are headed next. Sometimes the power of a plan is not even in the plan itself but in the *focused* thinking it takes to write it. You have had the opportunity to think about a variety of aspects in your business throughout this book and now it's all about getting a business and marketing plan to move forward. The fifth and final element is ACTION - without that all important element there are no results. This is where the follow up and follow through comes into the picture. This is where new habits are formed and new levels of discipline are enacted. Make it easier on yourself and share your plan with someone who will make the extra effort to hold you to your commitments. If you have dreams, set goals, learn how to achieve them, write a plan to get yourself there, and never take the actions – all of this will be for naught.

# SMART GOALS

Your plan starts with an understanding of how to write goals and the best guide to writing powerful goals is to double check that all your goals are SMART goals. SMART is an acronym for "Specific, Measurable, Achievable, Results-oriented, and has a Timeframe." When you take the extra effort to ensure your goals are SMART, you will have a clearer target, know how to get there, how long it should take you to get there and if you are there yet.

Specific implies you are clear about what the outcome will be when you accomplish the goal. Measureable is just how it sounds – there needs to be some kind of measurement to know if the goal has been achieved or not. One way to be more specific while including a measurement is to include where are you now "from" and where you will be when you reach your goal "to". This makes your goal more specific and must easier to measure than for example saying a blanket percentage increase like 10% increase in revenue. Without a specific "from… to…" measurement, you might have questions later like 10% of the monthly revenue or quarterly revenue or per client and does this include lost clients or just total new client's revenue?

Achievable is to remind you to set well-thought out goals based on past results or on projected outcomes using key indicators you've learned in the financial section like the 5 ways or profit breakeven. Write down goals that are thought out based on the seasonality or variability of your business – and do your best to avoid saying 50% improvement because that's what you want or that's what sounds good. Over time your ability to set achievable goals will continue to improve as you become more seasoned at planning and projecting but for now, do your best to put some thought into it and take your best estimate.

Results oriented means your goals need to have some sort of result in mind that you're looking to achieve. Just like being specific, you also want to make sure that the outcome and result is clearly stated so you will know what the point of that activity is and when you have achieve success in that goal.

Finally, Time frame is having a date to achieve it. This is commonly the element most often forgotten and can be the most valuable element because it helps with your focus and prioritization. Notice that just because you have a 90 day goal or one year goals doesn't mean that goal is going to take an entire year or an entire three months to complete. Think about your priorities and which goals you want to start and finish first. Give a time-frame that fits the difficulty, priority, and resources it will take to complete.

## ACTION PLAN

You have your SMART goals – and now it's time to discuss where you store them. Enter the ActionCOACH Weekly or Bi-Weekly Action Plan – a wonderful tool that will help you track your progress compared to your annual and 90 days goals all while keeping you focused on a weekly or bi-weekly basis all on one page, single-sided piece of paper. It will also give you a place to keep yourself proactively thinking about what you are doing to learn more through books, audio tapes or seminars that will help you achieve your tasks and goals faster and more effectively. The very bottom row even gives you a place to makes notes on how best you can utilize your coaching and what your coach can help you most with on your way to achieving the task and goals on the plan.

# WEEKLY ACTION PLAN – 2015

**ActionCOACH**
business coaching

| YEAR END GOALS | | Today's Date: |
| --- | --- | --- |

Name:

| | | | |
| --- | --- | --- | --- |
| | | | |

| 90-DAY PLAN | VALUE $$ |
| --- | --- |
| 1. Business Goal | |
| 2. Business Goal | |
| 3. Business Goal | |
| 4. Personal Goal | |

**THIS WEEK'S PLAN**

| Who | What Task | By When | Results Achieved |
| --- | --- | --- | --- |
| | | | |
| | | | |
| | | | |
| | | | |
| | | | |
| | | | |

**MY DEVELOPMENT PLAN**

| 1. Reading | |
| --- | --- |
| 2. Workshops | |
| 3. I Request Coaching on? | |

One of the best places to start is with your annual goals. On the action plan, you'll notice that there are four different boxes under year end goals. If this is your first time writing an action plan, it's best to start with at least one goal and grow from there. Over time you can do two or three at once, then once you reach a more advanced level you can try taking on four. Again, this is about being realistic and not taking on more than you know you can actually achieve, especially if you don't have a team or anyone to delegate some of these responsibilities to each week.

Start with one goal and pick a topic that is very important to the growth of your business. Typically, the first goal is always a financially driven goal, so it's on revenue or profit. Other areas you might choose as a second or third or fourth goal could be around some of the topics we've already discussed in previous chapters like marketing, measurement, systems, team, time, 5 ways, etc.

Let's start with an example of a financial goal to keep things simple. One way to look at what might be a financial goal is to go back and figure out how much you earned in revenue the previous year. Take into account where you want to be by next year using some of the projection tools and calculations you learned in the financial chapter like breakeven and target breakeven. Sometimes next year's goals are set solely based on where you need to get to breakeven or make some breakeven profitability where you are starting to pay yourself. For some businesses in their younger years, or years where they have been declining, this is a crucial place to get to financial safety. However, if you are already a growing business with consistent growth, start looking at the trends of how much and how fast you've been growing in the last year compared to the year before. Then we can start putting numbers into a backwards five ways to see if this is really possible in a year's time for your business and, if not, what it would take to get there. Remember to consider the different seasons in your business. Sometimes it is helpful to project your annual financials by projecting revenue for each of the four quarters and then taking a total.

Picture an Excel document with all the formulas already worked in, which you downloaded, and plug in where ever you would like your revenue to be one year from now. You would be able to plug in a certain level of sales dollars, a certain number of sales, how many customers you are looking at servicing in your business, and how many leads would that take to achieve those sales dollars. This will start allowing you to see what it's going to take in a one year period of time to accelerate your business to that goal level.

A lot of times, clients struggle with action plans because they have never made goals before, so being realistic about them can be a little challenging. Allowing us to coach and walk you through setting the goals, measuring and testing them each quarter, resetting the goals, and accurately assessing where you are compared to your annual basis, you will significantly improve at this skill, and goal setting a year or two from now will be a breeze. This process isn't about perfection; it is about thinking through what's realistic and getting an idea of what it will take moving forward to learn and master the skills.

Second, let's *focus* on your setting your 90 day goals. Again you can choose to start with just one 90 day goal or you can have up to three plus a personal goal. Start with your quarterly financial goal by entering where it says "business goal" the SMART goal for the next quarter's revenue increase based on your projections for the year. Let's say that your annual goal was to go from earning $50,000 in revenue the first year to earning a $150,000 in the second year—meaning you will more than double business earnings in the second year. Let's say the goal is set by December 31$^{st}$, 2015. Now, what is going to be the 90 day piece that you're going to take on? What's that financial goal look like? Maybe your business isn't very seasonal; it's completely balanced. Your $100,000 improvement averages out to a $25,000 improvement per quarter. In this case, you would write "From $12,500 per quarter to $37,500 per quarter revenue by March 31, 2015" where it says "1. Business Goal" on the action plan.

## SPECIFIC STRATEGIES

Now that you have your 90 day goal, you might have noticed the box to the right is still blank. That is where you will have room to note the different strategies you're going to use to accomplish that financial goal within the next 90 days. When you are *focused* on a goal tied to revenue or profit, a great place to start is by identifying specific 5 ways strategies to help you achieve that growth. You already learned that the five ways to increase revenue includes increasing leads, conversion rate of leads to customers, number of transactions, and average dollar sales. The additional five way also aids in improving your profitability by increasing your gross margin percentage.  With this in mind, one strategy to grow your revenue might be by impacting the number of leads by creating a target marketing campaign with measurement to know how well your marketing efforts are performing. Another might be to improve your conversion rate by mystery shopping your sales process and writing an improved script with training for answering the phone. A third strategy could be focused on increasing the number of transactions by getting a database of all your clients and putting in place a way to stay in touch with current offers. A fourth strategy could be to increase your average dollar sale by reviewing your pricing compared to competitors and starting a strategic price increase. These are all strategies that be written next to your revenue goal to create the action needed to drive revenue into your business over the next 90 days to achieve that $25,000 improvement.

You might have also noticed there is a 90 day goal place holder for a personal goal. There are probably some personal goals that would make you, as the owner or leader, more productive, less stressed and more effective when you achieved them. They could include working less hours, spending more time with family, getting healthier, or even continuing your education in some way. Stating personal goals is essential to aligning yourself with your future vision and dreams discussed in chapter 2 and allowing you to be the kind of future leader your business needs you to be.

# WEEKLY TASKS

Now that you have your annual goals and 90 days goals with strategies – it's time to identify what you will be working on in the next week or two weeks that will help you achieve those goals you've set. Coaching programs meet either on a weekly basis or on a bi-weekly basis so this will determine the frequency in which you will be setting weekly tasks on your action plan.

You will notice the first column is labeled "who" to remind you and encourage you to delegate task as frequently and as much as possible. The second column is where you will write the task you aim to work on that week. For example, if you are tackling your 90 day strategy of implementing a targeted marketing campaign, your weekly task might be to write out a detailed outline of your ideal, "A" client. The third column labeled "by when" is to help you set a timeframe based on when you can realistically complete the task. It will also remind you to connect this task with the calendar that you keep on a weekly basis – you know the one that you write all of your important appointments in - like when you are meeting with a client or your accountant. Now you can write this task in your calendar and treat it with the same level of respect. Finally the last column labeled "results achieved" is a place for you to write notes on the status of achieving that task or what was the outcome result achieved.

Below your weekly plan is your developmental plan where you will stay focused on learning and coaching that is connected to what you need to learn "just in time" to effectively execute what you've put on this week's plan. Remember, a lot of these tasks are ones you're learning and implementing for the first time. It is going to take some adjustment and may feel uncomfortable in the beginning. Our books, audio tapes, and seminars will expedite the speed of back office learning and allow you to get to a place where you feel more comfortable with your new skillsets, as well as allow you to get results at a much faster rate.

The last section of your action plan labeled "I request coaching on?" is a space to communicate with your greatest asset, your business coach, what tools, information, best practices, education, training, introductions, technology, etc. that would aid you in achieving your objectives that week.

# 90 DAY REVIEW

Imagine the last three months have flown by – you are taking focused action at a more accelerated rate than ever before and learning more than the last three years put together. What also tends to happen is you out perform your goals or you learn how realistic your goals were because for the first time you can see and measure the results. This is why it is so powerful for business owners to participate in a quarterly review process where they look back on the last three months to reflect on their top successes, the challenges they were able to overcome, what they learned from attending workshops or reading, how they did compared to their goals – and of course project where they are going next. ActionCOACH Tampa Bay facilitates a live workshop and private customized quarterly planning sessions to provide owners with a place to reset with their new found knowledge. They then set new SMART goals for the next 90 days and the cycle continues. *Focusing* on the plan and reviewing it regularly creates measureable results!

## CHAPTER 9
## KEY THOUGHTS

- ◎ Dream x Goal x Learn x Plan x Action
- ◎ SMART Goal Setting
- ◎ Focused Action Plan
- ◎ 90 Day Strategies
- ◎ Weekly Tasks
- ◎ Quarterly Review

## OMG! WHAT'S THE FOCUS?
## ACTION STEPS

1) _____

2) _____

3) _____

4) _____

5) _____

## CONTINUED
## THINKING

- ◎ One-Minute Manager – Blanchard
- ◎ Scaling Up – Harnish
- ◎ Thinking BIG – Tracy
- ◎ 4 Disciplines of Execution – McChesney and Covey
- ◎ Great By Choice – Collins and Hansen

# 10

## Accountability

*"Discipline is the bridge between goals and accomplishment."* – **Jim Rohn**

Isn't it amazing? Now you've got a plan. You've attended workshops, read books but the plans and research are not the end of things, instead it is just the beginning! Are you starting to see how important *focus* is in every portion of building your business?

When we surveyed our most successful clients, they came up with five things that they felt lead to their success. The first item was their mindset, keeping a positive outlook and making sure they remained aligned in their pursuit to achieve their end goals. Second was staying focused on the fundamentals in the business – understanding and reviewing their financials, marketing plan, 5 Ways, etc. Third was planning.  Having a plan and then updating their annual, quarterly, weekly and daily plan to keep the momentum going forward. Fourth was to BE continuous learners. Finally, and what most of our clients agree has helped them the most, is *accountability*. This is apparent in being a-count –able in their financials as well as holding them to the plans they agreed to complete. *Accountability* is the force that creates *focus* and keeps them on the path to success. It drives home the change in their businesses so they can quickly get *refocused* when off track.

We all have friends and family who listen to us and allow us to get away with whatever we want in life. But seeking *accountability* is a completely different methodology. Find people who challenge you. Find people who question you. People who ask you what you're doing and what you're going to learn. People who force you to take a hard look at your decisions. People who keep you on track and encourage you to drive home your dreams and goals. *Accountability* is truly about who will push you to succeed. Hire an ActionCOACH for your business growth strategy! Seek *accountability*!

## ACCOUNTABILITY PARTNERS – YOU AND YOUR COACH

Many people are quick to shoot you down, to tell you your ideas are stupid, that you will never achieve anything. Often we are too quick to put ourselves down. An accountability partner, your coach, will encourage you and push you in a positive way. They are your dream builders, not your dream destroyers. Someone who's got a vested interest and a listening ear, providing positive affirmations and encouragements in return, so you can make decisions with confidence, move in the right direction, and take the proper steps with more certainty, faith, and conviction.

Richard Nixon once said, *"How do I know what I think until I see what I say?"* Sometimes you'll find this for yourself. When you start to discuss something controversial or something about which you are passionate, you'll hear things come out of your mouth you didn't previously know you were thinking until the moment it's said.

If you're a business owner, who do you talk to? Frankly, your spouse does not want to hear it. They've had their own day and their own issues. Your friends won't get it. They're not going to challenge you, they're not going to encourage you in an authentic way. And you can't talk to your employees, because looking to them for guidance is not a very effective methodology. That's why it's good to have a coach, a *trusted advisor* for your business. You can get honest feedback and encouragement. With them, you are in a high trust, safe environment where you feel comfortable sharing your perspective. They will help you, not judge you. Everyone needs that.

Be consistent. Your business will not grow if you implement a plan one day and not use it again until four months later. Everything is a weekly, ongoing effort. We see it all the time. Business owners move at different speeds. The ones who effectively execute a plan every week have more remarkable results. It's about continuous momentum.

Step back. Think about yourself. What if you did follow through with the plan? Jim Rohn talked about a concept called the law of diminishing intent. When you first get an idea and are excited about implementing your idea, your intent to follow through is at its highest point. Perhaps you've developed your plan, you're going to implement changes and you've decided to meet with an ActionCOACH to get the support and accountability you know you need. But if you don't take action quickly, the intent will begin to diminish. By next week you're back in the "whirlwind" of your life and the intent is diminished greatly. A month from now you won't even remember the promises you made to yourself.

*"Plans are only good intentions unless they immediately degenerate into hard work."* - **Peter Drucker**.

So if you're going to capitalize on your intent, find something to do. Today. Tomorrow. Follow up. Follow through. Just get started. Let things unfold. Move forward. The right time is now!

# SEVEN MYTHS OF COACHING

**The 1st Myth**: <u>Every business is different.</u> Business owners say that all the time. Fact is, there's a lot of things businesses have in common. At the end of the day, everybody wants customers, revenue, and profit. How you come to those numbers is the same, no matter what industry or how long you've been in business.

**The 2nd Myth**: <u>Whoever helps you needs to have years' of experience and success in your specific industry.</u> If someone does not understand your industry, they can see the business from the outside perspective. They are not emotionally tied to how things have always been done. They can come up with new innovative, usually inexpensive ways to grow. This actually gives you an advantage over your competition because you are getting a different view of your business strategies.

**The 3rd Myth:** <u>Coaching does not help an experienced business person.</u> People tend to think that coaching is not useful after a certain period of time. There's a lot of undiscovered opportunities. Although you've slowly grown based on your experience, when you continuously learn and implement coaching, you speed up that process. You can then get more time and profitability out of actions you've already taken on a daily basis. Clients that put time and effort into coaching get the most out of it – measured in time away, revenue, profit and exit plan.

**The 4<sup>th</sup> Myth**: <u>I'm already successful, I'm already growing, why even take on a coach?</u> People think coaches bail out failing businesses, and that's all they are good for. No matter your success level, you still need improvement. Top performing Olympic athletes still receive coaching. Just because you are successful doesn't mean you reached your full potential. That's what coaches do!

**The 5th Myth**: <u>Business coaches are for start-ups or struggling businesses.</u> Unfortunately, start-up businesses are usually too distracted with marketing and branding that they do not realize a coach could help stabilize their business (not to mention that they are usually underfunded). As far as struggling businesses, most come for help when it is too late. They were too ashamed to get help earlier, but now they need it out of desperation. Unfortunately, struggling businesses cannot use coaching. Usually, they are too far gone. It all depends. Are you waiting until you're deep in debt? Don't. If you are starting to struggle, get help immediately before it is too late!

**The 6th Myth**: <u>Coaching takes up more time and money than the business can afford.</u> Coaching is not about taking up more time or money. It's about figuring out where you spend your time and money, that produces no return. It's about efficiency. Very quickly, the wheels will turn and you will work less hours, with more productivity, and you'll be making more of a return on your investment while actually enjoying the work.

**The 7th Myth**: <u>All coaches are the same.</u> No. Assume that, and you will miss out on the various  programs we have to offer. Remember, replace the "I Know" with curiosity and "isn't that interesting?" Ask questions and learn more.

# THREE OPTIONS

As a family business, we are absolutely passionate about helping people. Since we got involved with the *ActionCOACH Business System*, we wanted to articulate the key points most commonly used by businesses to succeed. It's tremendously rewarding for us to see those results too.

If a business owner asks, "Is this system for me?" we would tell them it really boils down to three options:

1. **Leave things the way they are.** You're successful on some level, and maybe that's fine. Maybe you can keep working slowly, but you will basically stay where you are.

2. **Get fired up**. "Man, there's some opportunities for the taking, and some books that need reading. I'm going to implement this plan, locate this reference, order fifteen books for tomorrow. Doggone it, I'm doing it on my own." That's a very high risk option. The reality remains, that option has been available to you since day one, and you have not done it. What are the chances you will do it now because you read one book?

3. **Try some professional help**. We'd love to help you. Studies show you will receive a return on your investment from coaching. An independent study with the University of Miami upon review of clients' financials, *ActionCOACH clients* received ten dollars of return for every dollar invested in coaching. 10:1 was the average return on investment.

*"The game has its ups and downs, but you can never lose focus of your individual goals and you can't let yourself be beat because of lack of effort."* - **Michael Jordan**

# CHAPTER 10
## KEY THOUGHTS

◎ Accountability Partners
◎ Create Change
◎ Failure to Participate
◎ Seven Myths

# OMG! WHAT'S THE FOCUS?
## ACTION STEPS

1) _____
2) _____
3) _____
4) _____
5) _____

## CONTINUED THINKING

◎ Drive – Pink
◎ Our Iceberg is Melting – Kotter
◎ The OZ Principle – Hickman and Smith
◎ How Did That Happen? – Connors and Smith
◎ The Business Coach - Sugars

# ABOUT THE AUTHORS

**Barb Kyes**
**Managing Partner**
**Executive and Business Coach**
**Assessment Specialist**

Barb has successfully incorporated the nurturing and caring traits that once made her a great nurse into her career as a business coach and executive leader.

Now, instead of diagnosing and treating patients she is assessing companies and coaching corporate leaders. Before ActionCOACH, Barb successfully operated 3 home-based businesses and as a consultant, wrote the business plan for a Seattle-based medical coding company to enter the Florida market. That company was later successfully sold by its owner based on its track-record of creating its national footprint. Barb also gathered the research and wrote the business plan for a local transitional housing thrift shop that serves as a funding source for the women in domestic violence situations. This facility is also a way that the women can obtain a work history and learn the skills that are necessary to put their lives back in order. Barb is the true entrepreneur of the team who can see both the big picture and the important details and has the persistence to achieve the company's vision and goals.

## Leader and Coach

As an innovative thinker and leader of one of the most successful coaching firms in the world, consistently among the top firms globally and in the U.S., she has been setting a standard and model for other coaches and business owners across the global organization. Barb and her team are continuous learners, bringing cutting edge ideas, best practices and opportunities to their clients of all sizes.

## Volunteer

In her spare time, Barb has volunteered her talents to help numerous nonprofits. She has also served in a leadership capacity with her local chambers of commerce, serving as founding chair women of the St. Petersburg Chamber of Commerce's Entrepreneurial Academy Alumni Association and a faculty member in the chamber's Master's Academy Program. She was also a perennial judge for the chamber's Small Business Awards and its Women of Distinction Business Awards. Barb was a finalist for 2010 and 2011 St. Petersburg Chamber Women of Distinction, Businesswoman of the Year. Barb has been nominated for the 2015 St. Petersburg Chamber Inspire Iconic Woman of the Year. Barb was asked to serve on the Tampa Bay Business Journal's Mentoring Monday, an annual event that mentors business women in 43 markets across the United States reaching 10,000 women on one day. Barb was named a finalist of the Tampa Bay Business Journal's 2010 Business Woman of the Year Award, which included over 300 nominations—the largest response since the awards began in 2004. Recently Barb has volunteered her time as a Rotarian in the Rotary of St. Petersburg organization and was elevated to the join the Board of Directors and Chairman of Membership for her 93 year old chapter in 2014.

**WHY Barb Loves Coaching...**

To Barb, the key to successful business coaching is building a strong connection with those she is coaching. Barb's always had an uncanny ability that seems like a sign on her forehead saying "you can talk to me" which she now uses to create a safe place for business leaders and family owned businesses to be candid about the undiscussed conflicts so the root of the challenge can finally get on the table to be resolved. Barb aims to make each and every one of her clients feel as though they are a part of her own family. That is why there is nothing more rewarding to Barb than watching her clients grow to new heights and have both personal and professional breakthroughs.

**Ford Kyes**

**Founding Partner**

**Executive and Business Coach**

**Presenter and Keynote Speaker**

As a corporate business leader, Ford gained valuable coaching experience by mentoring graduate students in hospital management and MBA programs for five different universities. Ford is the founding partner of the company and has achieved outstanding success for both large and small companies throughout his career. A graduate of Carnegie Mellon University's Master's program in management, Ford is passionate about helping individuals and businesses achieve their full potential by passing on his own business knowledge. Ford has been recognized as a Top 100 coach in ActionCOACH's global franchise of coaches and has served as a global trainer of new coaches in the franchise.

**Experience in the Healthcare**

Prior to launching ActionCOACH Tampa Bay, Ford served for six years as president and CEO of St. Anthony's Health Care in St. Petersburg, Fla. and Executive Vice President for the 10 Hospital, BayCare Health System. During his tenure, he made significant improvements in many areas, including a $40 million hospital renovation, the addition of a $37 million outpatient center and the successful development of five new businesses in joint ownership with physicians. Previously, as regional vice president of materials management for the BayCare Health System, he implemented numerous best practices that resulted in more than $30 million in savings per year for the health system.

**Ford as Your Coach**

Ford's unique skillset of engaging even the most lackluster crowds and converting it into a jovial learning environment makes him a sought after keynote speaker locally as well as nationally.  Ford's passion lies in helping businesses develop their knowledge, skills and confidence to implement the changes they need in order to achieve their dreams. He wants his clients to view him as a friend who is completely committed to their success in business and in life, but also as a coach who will hold them accountable to their commitments and goals. Ford finds the process of coaching that results in the learning and discovery to be the best part of his work. For him, watching his clients' businesses transform and grow is not only tremendously rewarding but also fun.

**Business Coach and Speaker**

**Certified Guerrilla Marketing Trainer and Coach**

**Small Business Owner**

Juliet is masterful in guiding business leaders to identify and strengthen their unique abilities, giving her clients a powerful competitive advantage. She then shows them how to communicate that Unique Selling Proposition in a way that conveys confidence and profit.

Juliet graduated from University of South Florida with a degree in Business Management with a minor in Marketing. She completed her degree at night while operating as a manager in a national retail store during the day. Juliet opened new locations and recruited teams over the 7 years she spent in retail. Even taking on a once failing team and converting it through hiring, firing and training a team that broke national customer service feedback records and winning her team and store numerous regional awards.

**Experience**

In 2011, Juliet attended the 10-day highly intensive training and certification process to become an ActionCOACH certified business coach. Within her first month, she had taken on 5 new clients, two of which went on to successfully sell their businesses a few years later. Her years of apprenticeship under other coaches allowed her to come out of the gates strong as a coach and presenter. Juliet then went on to become a Certified Guerrilla Marketing Trainer and Coach, affording her the unique opportunity to be trained by the late and great Father of Guerrilla Marketing himself, Jay Conrad Levinson, with a small group of elite business leaders in his home in Debary, Florida. Anyone can read

Jay Conrad Levinson's books but as the Father of *Guerrilla Marketing* said: "I know that 90% of those people will read it, love the ideas, and not do anything about it. They just don't have the ability to take action. Guerrilla Marketing is not a spectator sport, it is all about action. I revere companies like ActionCOACH because without these people much of what I write about and speak about would be for not because people won't do anything about it." Juliet uses her passion and experience for marketing to help companies create operational marketing plans and business plans that have successfully lead to obtaining business loans and lines of credit as well as helping to create marketing departments and recruiting marketing leadership.

**Leader and Small Business Owner**

In 2009, Juliet was nominated for the St. Petersburg Chamber of Commerce Young Professional of the Year award and nominated for the 2010 Tampa Bay Business Journal's Up and Comers award. Juliet has volunteered her talents for leadership, event promotion and marketing design to help a variety of nonprofits. She also donates her time and passion working with rescued dogs and cats at Pet Pal, a non-kill animal shelter. Through that passion for pets, in the fall of 2010 Juliet founded with her wife, Jennifer Kahler, a pet services and house cleaning company called Regal Pet Services. Since its opening, the business has doubled in growth year over year allowing Juliet to experience first-hand what it takes to start a business from scratch without any systems, structure and support that a franchise provides.

**Juliet as your Coach**

Juliet is most passionate about her work helping business owners. She understands that most business owners started their business to gain the freedom to work for themselves, at the hours they want, and to make more money than they would be earning working for someone else. However, somewhere along the way, business owners can lose freedom, and they end up working even harder than before for less money than they expected. Juliet wants to be the catalyst that business owners need to start proactively taking actions to achieve their dreams! Her goal is to help her clients feel excited and focused about their business by working smarter not harder. For Juliet, there is no greater reward than helping business owners achieve success and seeing their eyes light up with a passion for success.

# Free Resource Downloads

- IVVM Exercise - www.actioncoachtampabay.com/ivvm
- 6 Steps Mastery Checklist - www.actioncoachtampabay.com/six
- Vision – Mission – Culture Exercise - www.actioncoachtampabay.com/vmc
- Quick Time Study Exercise - www.actioncoachtampabay.com/time
- Default Calendar Tool - www.actioncoachtampabay.com/calendar
- Eat The Frog – MI5 Tool - www.actioncoachtampabay.com/frog
- Projection Tool - www.actioncoachtampabay.com/pro
- 5 Ways Tool - www.actioncoachtampabay.com/five
- USP and Guarantee Exercise - www.actioncoachtampabay.com/niche
- Marketing Measurement Tool - www.actioncoachtampabay.com/measure
- Quick DISC Quiz - www.actioncoachtampabay.com/disc
- Objections Exercise - www.actioncoachtampabay.com/object
- 4 Areas of Systems List Tool - www.actioncoachtampabay.com/four
- Dream Builder Exercise - www.actioncoachtampabay.com/dream
- Big 3 Financial Documents Examples - www.actioncoachtampabay.com/three

# Recommended Reading

## Chapter 1
- Focus – Goleman
- How Full is Your Bucket – Rath
- Five Major Pieces to the Life Puzzle – Rohn
- 7 Habits of Highly Effective People – Covey
- It's Your Ship – Captain Abrashoff

## Chapter 2
- The Business Coach – Sugars
- Built to Last – Collins
- The Last Lecture – Pausch
- The Answer – Assaraf & Smith
- Start with Why – Sinek

## Chapter 3
- Billionaire in Training – Sugars
- The Cashflow Quadrant – Kiyosaki
- 7 Habits of Highly Effective People – Covey
- Mastering the Rockefeller Habits – Harnish
- The Compounding Effect – Hardy

## Chapter 4
- Instant Cashflow – Sugars
- Instant Profit – Sugars
- The Ultimate Blueprint for an Insanely Successful Business – Cunningham

## Chapter 5
- Guerrilla Marketing – Levinson
- Instant Leads – Sugars
- Purple Cow – Godin
- Instant Advertising – Sugars
- Buying Customers – Sugars

## Chapter 6
- Instant Sales – Sugars
- Little Gold Book of Yes! Attitude – Gitomer
- Go for No – Waltz and Fenton
- Little Red Book of Selling – Gitomer
- The Platinum Rule – Dr. Alessandra

## Chapter 7
- Instant Systems – Sugars
- Instant Scripts Ebook – Sugars
- Instant Testing & Measuring Ebook – Sugars
- Six Sigma for Dummies – Gygi, DeCarlo and Williams
- E-Myth Revisited – Gerber

## Chapter 8
- Instant Team Building – Sugars
- Who – Smart and Street
- First Break All The Rules – Buckingham
- Gung Ho – Blanchard
- Speed of Trust – Covey
- What Got You Here Won't Get You There – Goldsmith

## Chapter 9
- One-Minute Manager – Blanchard
- Scaling Up – Harnish
- Thinking BIG – Tracy
- 4 Disciplines of Execution – McChesney and Covey
- Great By Choice – Collins and Hansen

## Chapter 10
- Drive – Pink
- Our Iceberg is Melting – Kotter
- The OZ Principle – Hickman and Smith
- How Did That Happen? – Connors and Smith
- The Business Coach – Sugars

# Final Thoughts

At ActionCOACH Tampa Bay, we're not just a team of business coaches. We're a family of dynamic business professionals. Our coaches, Ford, Barb and Juliet Kyes, have over 55 years of combined experience working in the Tampa Bay business community. We have the real life experience and knowledge to guide your company to success.

ActionCOACH Tampa Bay is dedicated to helping grow businesses and improving the community by spreading proactive leadership skills and proven business strategies. Our family is proud to work together to bring you the highest quality business coaching in the Tampa Bay area and beyond.

The ActionCOACH Tampa Bay firm is ready to take you and your business to the next level. Whether that entails taking your company public or moving to a national or international scale, our skilled team guarantees to help you reach your professional and business goals.

Reach out, see if we can help you. We have already worked with over seventy different types of businesses in our area since 2007. *ActionCOACH* is a global franchise. We really know what we're doing, and we know beyond a shadow of a doubt that this works. We wish you the best in your endeavors.

Pick up the phone. Call us. If you're not in the Tampa Bay Area, that's okay. Call us. We'll find a way to get you the assistance you deserve. Call 727-786-2900. Middle of the night? It's okay, we've got answering machines. We'll follow up the very next business day.